Japanese Character Writing

by Hiroko Chiba, PhD and Vincent Grépinet

A Wiley Brand

Japanese Character Writing For Dummies®

Published by: **John Wiley & Sons, Inc.,** 111 River Street, Hoboken, NJ 07030-5774, www.wiley.com

Copyright © 2020 by John Wiley & Sons, Inc., Hoboken, New Jersey

Published simultaneously in Canada

No part of this publication may be reproduced, stored in a retrieval system or transmitted in any form or by any means, electronic, mechanical, photocopying, recording, scanning or otherwise, except as permitted under Sections 107 or 108 of the 1976 United States Copyright Act, without the prior written permission of the Publisher. Requests to the Publisher for permission should be addressed to the Permissions Department, John Wiley & Sons, Inc., 111 River Street, Hoboken, NJ 07030, (201) 748-6011, fax (201) 748-6008, or online at http://www.wiley.com/go/permissions.

Trademarks: Wiley, For Dummies, the Dummies Man logo, Dummies.com, Making Everything Easier, and related trade dress are trademarks or registered trademarks of John Wiley & Sons, Inc., and may not be used without written permission. All other trademarks are the property of their respective owners. John Wiley & Sons, Inc., is not associated with any product or vendor mentioned in this book.

LIMIT OF LIABILITY/DISCLAIMER OF WARRANTY: WHILE THE PUBLISHER AND AUTHOR HAVE USED THEIR BEST EFFORTS IN PREPARING THIS BOOK, THEY MAKE NO REPRESENTATIONS OR WARRANTIES WITH RESPECT TO THE ACCURACY OR COMPLETENESS OF THE CONTENTS OF THIS BOOK AND SPECIFICALLY DISCLAIM ANY IMPLIED WARRANTIES OF MERCHANTABILITY OR FITNESS FOR A PARTICULAR PURPOSE. NO WARRANTY MAY BE CREATED OR EXTENDED BY SALES REPRESENTATIVES OR WRITTEN SALES MATERIALS. THE ADVICE AND STRATEGIES CONTAINED HEREIN MAY NOT BE SUITABLE FOR YOUR SITUATION. YOU SHOULD CONSULT WITH A PROFESSIONAL WHERE APPROPRIATE. NEITHER THE PUBLISHER NOR THE AUTHOR SHALL BE LIABLE FOR DAMAGES ARISING HEREFROM.

For general information on our other products and services, please contact our Customer Care Department within the U.S. at 877-762-2974, outside the U.S. at 317-572-3993, or fax 317-572-4002. For technical support, please visit https://hub.wiley.com/community/support/dummies.

Wiley publishes in a variety of print and electronic formats and by print-on-demand. Some material included with standard print versions of this book may not be included in e-books or in print-on-demand. If this book refers to media such as a CD or DVD that is not included in the version you purchased, you may download this material at http://booksupport.wiley.com. For more information about Wiley products, visit www.wiley.com.

Library of Congress Control Number: 2019953292

ISBN 978-1-119-47543-9 (pbk); ISBN 978-1-119-47545-3 (ebk); ISBN 978-1-119-47534-7 (ebk)

Manufactured in the United States of America

V10017714_022020

Table of Contents

Introduction

Every language has its own journey and stories. This book introduces the stories of the Japanese language through the practice of kanji. More than 1,500 years ago, kanji came to Japan from China through Korea. It's a meaning-based script — that is, each kanji represents a meaning. Kanji is not only an essential part of the Japanese language, but is also used as a medium for art such as calligraphy. Whatever your degree of interest in Japanese language and culture, you will feel the joy of setting foot in a new world by learning kanji. You may have heard that kanji is complicated and difficult to learn. Although it is true that one cannot master kanji overnight, you will find the learning process quite enjoyable.

About This Book

This book is intended for people who have absolutely no prior knowledge of kanji. However, it is also useful for those who have learned Japanese but want to polish their kanji.

In this book, you will learn 105 characters of Japanese kanji. Each kanji is introduced with a story related to the kanji along with examples of how it's used. There will be plenty of spaces (which look like square boxes) for you to practice the target kanji. Remember to follow the stroke order (the order for drawing lines in each kanji). Once you get a general sense of how the lines are ordered, you can speed up your writing, which will make learning kanji faster and more efficient. Before you start browsing kanji introduced in this book, here is some helpful information to keep in mind:

>> **Hiragana annotations (ruby).** We've placed the hiragana annotations above most of the kanji used in the description, in case you already know hiragana. For example, the kanji 山 for "mountain" will be displayed with hiragana やまabove it, so the result will look like this:

>> **Selection of kanji.** The choice of a hundred five basic kanji is very subjective. We selected the ones that we thought were the most useful for everyday living, for understanding leaflets, signs, menus, and so on.

>> **Readings (pronunciations) of kanji.** For most kanji, there are two types of readings: *on'yomi* and *kun'yomi* readings. *On'yomi* is an appropriation of the original Chinese sound and *kun'yomi* is often called Japanese reading, which indicates that the word is of Japanese origin. This system is explained in more detail in Chapter 1. Some of the kanji we've selected here have more readings, but we've presented the most common ones.

>> **Kanji compounds.** Kanji may be used independently with grammatical endings in hiragana. You will also see multiple kanji characters in one word. In this book, we call these multiple-kanji words "kanji compounds."

I also use a few conventions in this book to help your reading go smoothly:

>> In many places throughout this book, Japanese terms appear in two forms: as Japanese scripts (like what you would read if you were in Japan) and as romanized forms of words (which appear in *italics* so you can easily find them in the text). The official term for romanized Japanese is **rōmaji** (rohh-mah-jee). Although, in many cases, it is easy to figure out how to pronounce rōmaji, when you are not sure of the pronunciation of a rōmaji sound, refer to Table 1-2, 1-3, and 1-4.

>> Following each Japanese term, its meaning or English equivalent is provided within a pair of parentheses.

>> Conventionally, in kanji dictionaries that are written for English speakers, the pronunciation of Chinese origin is printed in uppercase letters, but the words of Japanese origin are written in lowercase. We will follow that convention in this book.

Note: Grammar points are not covered in this book, but you can learn more about Japanese grammar in *Japanese For Dummies*!

Foolish Assumptions

This is an exercise book for writing Japanese kanji. We created this book assuming the following:

>> You know a little Japanese, but you never had time to study kanji characters.

>> You do not know anything about Japanese, but its written form fascinates you.

>> You have already done some Japanese writing, but you have forgotten it and want to practice more.

>> You are interested in calligraphy.

Icons Used in This Book

The following icons will appear periodically in the book to highlight important points to help you succeed in your mission of mastering kanji.

REMEMBER

This icon will point out particularly important information to commit to memory.

TIP

Be on the lookout for this icon to get helpful pointers on how to form the characters with the greatest ease and efficiency.

WARNING

This icon flags some of the most common mistakes that people tend to make.

Where to Go from Here

If you're really excited to jump into the practice exercises, you can skip over Chapters 1 and 2 and go straight to the practice. However, you will find the information in the first two chapters helpful as you begin your kanji practice.

REMEMBER

When you practice kanji, remember the following tips:

>> Make sure to follow the stroke order.

>> Write each kanji or kanji word many times to solidify your kanji memory.

>> As you practice, it's important to say kanji words out loud, so can hear the sounds. This will also assist with your memory.

>> When you are not sure of the pronunciation of rōmaji, refer to Chapter 1.

>> Use the extra practice sheets at the end of this book as needed.

>> There are variations of radicals, but we presented the one used in the kanji introduced in this book.

>> Enjoy!

After finishing this book, you will have a pretty good idea of how kanji is generally constructed and how to write it. You will then be able to embark on your kanji learning in different ways by employing the skills you acquire through this book. You will find it very exciting to figure out how to write and learn new kanji. This book provides basic examples of how to use each kanji, but there are many more kanji words you can pick up. I recommend that you get a notebook (or notebooks) just for kanji practice, and that you browse and review kanji you have studied whenever you have time; this will reinforce and solidify your kanji memory. Although it can be very enjoyable, mastering kanji takes patience and a lot of practice, so be proud of your accomplishments!

Chapter **1**

Wrapping Your Head around Japanese Writing and Pronunciation

This chapter introduces basic information about Japanese sounds and the three writing scripts: kanji, hiragana, and katakana. It is essential for you to know how the Japanese sound system works to be able to learn how to pronounce kanji correctly. You will find that kanji plays an important role in the Japanese language. Foundational information in this chapter will provide context to begin to learn kanji.

Brief History of Three Writing Scripts: Kanji, Hiragana, and Katakana

Three writing scripts? It may seem very strange to have three different writing scripts in one language. Let me give a brief history illustrating why the Japanese language needed the three types of characters.

Taking a cue from Chinese writing — Kanji

For a long time, the Japanese language did not have a writing system. It was not until the 5th century that kanji (Chinese characters), the writing of "Han China" (pronounced "kan" in Japanese), was introduced into the Japanese archipelago via Korea.

This does not mean, however, that Japanese people did not communicate with one another until the 5th century. Japanese already existed in its oral form. When Chinese characters, kanji, were introduced, there was a difficulty. The grammatical structure of Japanese is radically different from that of Chinese. In addition, phonologically speaking, Japanese is a syllabic language in which one syllable corresponds to one sound that does not indicate any meaning on its own. In the Chinese language, each character is associated with a single sound and a single meaning. So people needed to figure out how Japan's indigenous language could adopt this writing system. As you can imagine, it was not an easy task!

Initially, the Chinese texts, mainly Buddhist, were studied and assimilated as such. Any well-trained scholars at that time knew how to write and read in classical Chinese, which was called *kanbun* (Han style text). Reading this kind of text requires some intellectual effort. Diacritical signs were invented to indicate the order in which one had to read the kanji so that the Chinese text would conform to Japanese grammatical structure.

As far as pronunciation was concerned, attempts were made to reproduce the Chinese sounds with varying degrees of success, resulting in the approximation of the original sounds. At the same time, kanji was applied to write original Japanese words based on the meanings, not the Chinese pronunciations, of the kanji. This explains why most kanji have 音読み *onyomi* (an approximation of the Chinese pronunciation), and 訓読み *kunyomi* (the original Japanese pronunciation). For example, the kanji, 人 (person), has three different pronunciations in Japanese: JIN, NIN, and hito.

Creating writing scripts better suited to Japanese — hiragana and katakana

By the end of the Heian period (794–1185), Japanese people had invented two other writing scripts that fit the Japanese language better. These two writing scripts are collectively called *kana* and are derived from kanji. The original forms of kana were initially used to indicate the pronunciation of Chinese words.

These two kana scripts are called hiragana and katakana. Hiragana was derived from the simplification of some kanji in Japanese cursive writing. This writing was widely used by women of the aristocracy. In the 11th century, two women, Murasaki Shikibu and Sei Shōnagon, wrote their internationally recognized masterpieces, *The Tale of Genji* and *The Pillow Book*, respectively, using mainly this writing. As for Japanese men at that time, they reserved hiragana for their personal correspondence. Katakana was also created from a part of the kanji.

TIP

We still use hiragana to indicate grammatical parts of words such as verb endings, functional words, and so forth. For instance, the kanji for "white" is 白い with the hiragana い being the grammatical ending for an adjective. But katakana is typically used to transliterate *loan words* — words imported from other languages ピアノ/piano, for example, is an imported word and thus is written in katakana.

We've rushed through the history of the three writing scripts in Japanese, but I hope you get the idea!

A FOURTH WRITING SCRIPT?

Some people might say there are four writing scripts in Japanese. What is the fourth one? It's called *rōmaji*, literally Roman letters, which transcribe Japanese sounds into Latin letters, such as "Tokyo." The romanization of words can been seen in signs, logos, posters, train stations and other public apparatuses and it is part of our everyday life. So, yes we could say it's used as one of the writing scripts.

Pronouncing Japanese Sounds

Japanese sounds are very easy to pronounce because each syllable is simple and clear. There are only five vowels: a, i, u, e, and o (pronounced *ah, ee, oo, eh, oh*). Including these vowels, there are 46 basic sounds. Each hiragana and katakana corresponds to one sound. A sound consists of one consonant and one vowel such as *ka* [kah] (*k* as the consonant and *a* as the vowel) except for ん *n*, which is the only stand-alone consonant in Japanese.

Take a look at Table 1-1, which has the basic 46 hiragana. The pronunciation of each sound is indicated in *rōmaji*. There are some missing sounds, but don't worry — it's not a mistake! These sounds do not exist in contemporary Japanese. You have to read from the right column to the left column and from top to bottom in each column.

Table 1-1   Hiragana Table

n	w-	r-	y-	m-	h-	n-	t-	s-	k-		
ん n	わ wa	ら ra	や ya	ま ma	は ha	な na	た ta	さ sa	か ka	あ a	-a
		り ri		み mi	ひ hi	に ni	ち chi	し shi	き ki	い i	-i
		る ru	ゆ yu	む mu	ふ fu	ぬ nu	つ tsu	す su	く ku	う u	-u
		れ re		め me	へ he	ね ne	て te	せ se	け ke	え e	-e
	を (w)o	ろ ro	よ yo	も mo	ほ ho	の no	と to	そ so	こ ko	お o	-o

In this book, you don't have to know katakana, but for your information, Table 1-2 provides basic sounds in hiragana and katakana.

Table 1-2   Basic Hiragana and Katakana

Rōmaji	Pronunciation	Hiragana	Katakana
a	ah	あ	ア
i	ee	い	イ
u	oo	う	ウ
e	eh	え	エ
o	oh	お	オ
ka	kah	か	カ
ki	kee	き	キ
ku	koo	く	ク
ke	keh	け	ケ
ko	koh	こ	コ
sa	sah	さ	サ
shi	shee	し	シ
su	soo	す	ス
se	seh	せ	セ

(continued)

Table 1-2 *(continued)*

Rōmaji	Pronunciation	Hiragana	Katakana
so	*soh*	そ	ソ
ta	*tah*	た	タ
chi	*chee*	ち	チ
tsu	*tsoo*	つ	ツ
te	*teh*	て	テ
to	*toh*	と	ト
na	*nah*	な	ナ
ni	*nee*	に	ニ
nu	*noo*	ぬ	ヌ
ne	*neh*	ね	ネ
no	*noh*	の	ノ
ha	*hah*	は	ハ
hi	*hee*	ひ	ヒ
fu	*foo*	ふ	フ
he	*heh*	へ	ヘ
ho	*hoh*	ほ	ホ
ma	*mah*	ま	マ
mi	*mee*	み	ミ
mu	*moo*	む	ム
me	*meh*	め	メ
mo	*moh*	も	モ
ya	*yah*	や	ヤ
yu	*yoo*	ゆ	ユ
yo	*yoh*	よ	ヨ
ra	*rah*	ら	ラ
ri	*ree*	り	リ
ru	*roo*	る	ル
re	*reh*	れ	レ
ro	*roh*	ろ	ロ
wa	*wah*	わ	ワ
(w)o	*oh*	を	ヲ
n	*n*	ん	ン

Making Variations of Sounds

We need some additional sounds to be able to write all of the Japanese sounds we utter. We can make the rest of Japanese sounds using little tricks!

Two diacritical marks

In addition to the basic 46 sounds, there are variations of these sounds. First, I will show you how to make variations using two diacritical marks: two short dashes (") called *tenten* and a small circle (°) called *maru*.

By adding (”) to the upper-right corner of a **kana** character that starts with the consonant **k**, **s**, **t**, **h**, or **f**, you can make that consonant "voiced." For example, か represents *ka* (kah), while が represents *ga* (gah). So you can convert **k** to **g**, **s** to **z**, and **t** to **d** by using (" "). Strangely, **h** and **f** are turned into **b**. Also notice that じ and ぢ are both pronounced **ji** (jee), and ず and づ are both pronounced **zu** (zoo). (However, **ji** and **zu** are almost always represented by じ and ず, respectively.) Table 1-3 shows a comprehensive list of these variations. The pronunciation of each sound is indicated in the parentheses.

Table 1-3   Voiced Sounds and "P" Sounds

p	b	d/j	z/j	g	
ぱ pa	ば ba	だ da	ざ za	が ga	a
(pah)	(bah)	(dah)	(zah)	(gah)	
ぴ pi	び bi	ぢ ji	じ ji	ぎ gi	i
(pee)	(bee)	(jee)	(jee)	(gee)	
ぷ pu	ぶ bu	づ zu	ず zu	ぐ gu	u
(poo)	(boo)	(zoo)	(zoo)	(goo)	
ぺ pe	べ be	で de	ぜ ze	げ ge	e
(peh)	(beh)	(deh)	(zeh)	(geh)	
ぽ po	ぼ bo	ど do	ぞ zo	ご go	o
(poh)	(boh)	(doh)	(zoh)	(goh)	

TIP

To understand voiced and unvoiced sounds, say **k** and **g** while lightly touching your throat. You feel a vibration only when you say **g**, even though you're doing largely the same thing with your mouth when you say **k**, right? Linguists call vibrationless sounds such as **k**, **p**, **t**, and **s**, *unvoiced* sounds, and sounds that do vibrate, such as **g**, **b**, **d**, and **z**, *voiced* sounds.

A small circle (°) in the upper-right corner of a **kana** character makes a **p** sound. This applies only to **h** or **f** sounds. An example is ぷ *pu*.

Long vowels

The five basic vowels — **a**, **i**, **u**, **e**, and **o** — can be elongated. For example, you can think of a short vowel as having one beat like a quarter note in music, but a long vowel having two beats like a half note. Long vowels have the same sound as short vowels, but you just draw out the sound for a moment longer. In this book, the long vowels are represented by using single letters with a bar (¯) over them, as in ā, ī, ū, ē, and ō. For example, the kanji word for *mother* is お母さん *okāsan*.

Small ya, yu, yo

A small-sized や (**ya**) (*yah*), ゆ (**yu**) (*yoo*), or よ (**yo**) (*yoh*) after a syllable with a vowel **i** (ee) makes contracted sounds. Basically you replace **i** with **y**. But this is not about lowercase or uppercase; you just need to make the size of the character smaller by 50 to 75 percent. For example, き (**ki**) (kee) followed by the small-sized や yields きゃ *kya* (kyah).

The same applies to katakana. The size difference can be difficult to see in print, but you will gradually get used to it. Here is an example from the writing section. The kanji for *hundred* is 百, which is pronounced ひゃく *hyaku* (hyah-koo). Table 1-4 shows how each sound with a small *ya*, *yu*, and *yo* is written. The pronunciation of each sound is indicated in parentheses.

Table 1-4   Small *ya, yu, yo*

きゃ kya	きゅ kyu	きょ kyo
(kyah)	(kyoo)	(kyoh)
しゃ sha	しゅ shu	しょ sho
(shah)	(shoo)	(shoh)
ちゃ cha	ちゅ chu	ちょ cho
(chah)	(choo)	(choh)
にゃ nya	にゅ nyu	にょ nyo
(nyah)	(nyoo)	(nyoh)
ひゃ hya	ひゅ hyu	ひょ hyo
(hyah)	(hyoo)	(hyoh)
みゃ mya	みゅ myu	みょ myo
(myah)	(myoo)	(myoh)
りゃ rya	りゅ ryu	りょ ryo
(ryah)	(ryoo)	(ryoh)
ぎゃ gya	ぎゅ gyu	ぎょ gyo
(gyah)	(gyoo)	(gyoh)
じゃ ja	じゅ ju	じょ jo
(jah)	(joo)	(joh)
ぢゃ ja	ぢゅ ju	ぢょ jo
(jah)	(joo)	(joh)
びゃ bya	びゅ byu	びょ byo
(byah)	(byoo)	(byoh)
ぴゃ pya	ぴゅ pyu	ぴょ pyo
(pyah)	(pyoo)	(pyoh)

WARNING

When you speak, it's important to make a clear distinction between small *ya, yu,* and *yo* and regular *ya, yu,* and *yo.* For example, *byōin* refers to a hospital, but *biyōin* refers to a beauty salon. When you want to go to a hospital, you might arrive at a beauty salon if you don't carefully pronounce the word!

Small tsu

In Japanese, double consonants such as *tt* or *pp* are written with small つ **tsu** and indicated by a brief pause. You don't really pronounce a sound. For example, the kanji for "eight hundred" is 八百 *happyaku.*

When to Use Kanji

As I mentioned, there are two other writing scripts in Japanese, hiragana and katakana. These scripts seem simpler and can transcribe any sound into Japanese. You may therefore have this burning question: Why do we need a complicated writing script like kanji?

There are a few reasons why kanji is convenient and useful. Kanji is often used for "content words" such as nouns, adjectives, verbs, and adverbs. By using kanji, we don't get confused with homonyms. For example, *dento* can refer to either electric lights or tradition. Kanji can clarify this instantly. In any case, certain aspects of Japanese grammar are expressed in hiragana.

TIP

When you speak, the context and pitch (high or low) in the word can also give someone cues regarding what word you are using.

Kanji can also economize a sentence and provide the meaning of the word without you completely sounding it out. Let's compare the following two sentences. The first is in kanji, while the second uses all hiragana.

新幹線を使うと、東京から京都まで2時間半で行けます。

しんかんせんをつかうと、とうきょうからきょうとまでにじかんはんでいけます。

Both sentences translate as, "If you use a bullet train, you can get to Kyoto from Tokyo in 2.5 hours." But the all-hiragana version is quite lengthy, and you need to sound it out to process the meaning of the sentence. The kanji version is more concise. The longer a sentence gets, the more kanji becomes helpful.

TIP

Kanji is aesthetically ingrained in Japanese culture. One of the most notable art forms is calligraphy. Beautiful writing with a brush and ink has been appreciated for many centuries since being introduced from China. Nowadays, you can get a *fudepen*, which is a brush-type pen that allows you to write calligraphy without the hassle of a traditional brush. You can try brush strokes with it and experience the feel of brush writing. But there is nothing like real brush writing, of course!

Chapter **2**

Exploring the Nature of Japanese Kanji

In this chapter, we explore the essentials of kanji, and also go over the mechanism of kanji to facilitate your kanji learning. This chapter provides information to help you recognize the parts of kanji, to understand how each kanji should be constructed, and to write a beautifully balanced kanji!

Getting to Know the Four Types of Kanji

When you look at kanji, they might appear to be just a bunch of lines creating a shape. But there is a useful way to categorize kanji into roughly four types, based on the way they're formed:

» Pictographs

» Simple ideographs

» Compound ideographs

» Phonetic-ideographic characters

 How many kanji do you have to know to read a Japanese newspaper or magazine? The Japanese government designates 2,136 commonly used kanji, called *jōyōkanji*.

REMEMBER

Pictographs

Some kanji are pictographs that are visual representations of things. In Japanese, they are called 象形文字 *shōkēmoji* (literally, characters that represent things). There are not many of them, however. A little over ten percent of *jōyōkanji* fall into this category. These kanji serve as fundamental constituents in many other kanji. Here are some examples of pictographs.

Mountain

Tree

Moon

Simple ideographs

Some kanji express abstract concepts such as numbers and locations. They are called 指示文字 *shijimoji*, which means "letters to indicate." Here are some examples.

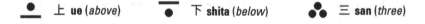

上 **ue** (*above*)   下 **shita** (*below*)   三 **san** (*three*)

The horizontal lines in kanji show the base line. For example, the kanji for "above" has lines above the horizontal line, while the kanji for "below" has lines under the horizontal line. The last example indicates "three" by drawing three lines.

Compound ideographs

The kanji created by combining two or more simple kanji are called 会意文字 *kaiimoji* (combined meanings). Here are some examples.

木 (tree) + 木 (tree) → 林 (tree and tree makes "woods")

日 (sun) + 月 (moon) → 明るい (sun and moon makes "bright")

人 (person) + 木 (tree) → 休む (person next to a tree makes "to rest")

Phonetic-ideographic characters

The next category of kanji is called 形声文字 *kēsēmoji*, which literally means "letters of shapes and voices/sounds." This is the largest group of kanji despite the common misconception that kanji are mostly pictographic or ideographic. These kanji are constructed with a part that shows a meaning and another that indicates sound. Take a look at some examples.

Part that shows a meaning	sound	kanji	on'yomi	meaning
日 (sun, day)	寺*ji* (temple)	時	*ji*	time
扌,手 (hand)	寺*ji* (temple)	持	*ji*	to carry

Both of these kanji, 時 and 持, sound the same because they have the same sound part!

REMEMBER

You might hear that there are six types of kanji in Japanese, but for this book, I only introduce the most common categories.

On'yomi versus Kun'yomi Readings

When Chinese characters came from China via Korea more than 1,500 years ago, mainly in Chinese religious texts, the Japanese language already existed, but it did not have a writing system. The Chinese writing system was adopted to translate the spoken language into a written form. This process, however, was not so easy because the Chinese and Japanese languages had very different linguistic structures. The solution to this problem was to create a dual pronunciation system: one that applied a Japanese word to a kanji that carried the same meaning (*kun'yomi*), and another that kept the original Chinese readings (*on'yomi*).

The Chinese readings are generally used to make kanji compounds, words with multiple kanji. Although we say Chinese readings, some of the readings may not sound like Chinese to speakers of contemporary Chinese. When they encountered kanji, Japanese people may not have heard Chinese sounds perfectly. And the Chinese language has evolved since then as well. You may also see multiple *on'yomi* because the adaptation of the same kanji took place during different periods. That's why Japanese kanji have become somewhat complicated!

Let's look at one example from the practice section. The *on'yomi* for 人 (person, people) is JIN or NIN, while *kun'yomi* is "hito." Keep in mind that there are some kanji that only have *kun'yomi* or *on'yomi*.

TIP

In kanji dictionaries that are written for English speakers, uppercase letters often indicate *on'yomi*, whereas lowercase letters are used to show *kun'yomi*.

Okurigana

If you have studied Japanese grammar, you may know some of the verb, adjective, and other conjugations. Many of the conjugated words are written in a mixture of kanji and hiragana. The hiragana part is called "*okurigana*." For example, 行く *iku* (to go) consists of the kanji, 行 (kanji for "go") and hiragana く. The く is the *okurigana* in this word. When you learn kanji, it's very important to be mindful about what part is written in kanji. The *okurigana* part is unique to each kanji, so you have to know it. Here are some more examples.

Verbs:

食べる *taberu* (to eat)

話します *hanashimasu* (to speak)

見ません *mimasen* (to not see) negative form

Adjectives:

高い *takai* (high)

大きくない *ōkikunai* (not big) negative form

TIP

These grammatical endings written in hiragana are explained in *Japanese For Dummies,* 3rd Edition, if you would like to investigate more.

Kanji compounds

Words that contain multiple kanji are called "kanji compounds." In a kanji compound, we typically apply *on'yomi* to each kanji. For example, 外国 *gai-koku* (foreign country) has two kanji to make up the word in which *on'yomi* is employed. However, there are kanji compounds that consist of just *kun'yomi* or a mixture of *on'yomi* and *kun'yomi*. Here are some examples:

on'yomi + on'yomi   音楽 on-gaku (music)

kun'yomi + kun'yomi   花見 hana-mi (flower viewing)

on'yomi + kun'yomi   毎年 mai-toshi (every year)

kun'yomi + on'yomi   夕飯 yū-han (supper, dinner)

Sound shifts in kanji compounds

Some compound words go through sound shifts within the compound. There are kanji compounds in which the initial unvoiced syllable of the non-initial kanji becomes voiced (indicated by the diacritical mark with two dots). For example, 百 *hyaku* (hundred) is pronounced *byaku* after 三 *san* (three), so 三百 is read *san-byaku*; the *h* becomes *b* (voiced) in the compound. There are also compound words in which small *tsu* takes over some sounds. For example, 回 *kai* is a counter for frequency, such as once, twice, and so on. After adding 一*ichi* (one) to it, 一回 is pronounced いっかい *ikkai*. Although these are not uncommon phonological behaviors, there are no clear rules for these sound shifts. But if you remember each one when you encounter a sound shift, it won't be so hard! Here are some more examples.

Unvoiced → voiced

花 *hana* (flower) + 火 *hi* (fire) → 花火 *hana-bi* (fireworks)

手 *te* (hand) + 紙 *kami* (paper) → 手紙 *te-gami* (letter)

Changing to small *tsu*

出 *shutsu* (to come out) + 世 *se* (world) → 出世 *shusse* (successful career)

別 *betsu* (separate) + 館 *kan* (building, hall) → 別館 *bekkan* (annex)

What Are Kanji Radicals?

You may be wondering what is meant by *kanji radicals.* The word "radical" is from the Latin word meaning "root"; it indicates a root part of a word. In Japanese kanji, it is a part tied to the meaning of the kanji. As discussed earlier, typically there is more than one part in one kanji. Some kanji may look complicated, and if you look at each one closely, you may be intrigued by its intricate structure. Radicals are called 部首 *bushu* in Japanese and are often associated with the meaning of the kanji. Some of them are stand-alone kanji that can be used as independent characters, whereas other radicals are used only as parts of other kanji. There are 214 radicals in total with some variations. As you look at the following kanji, think about what they have in common.

海 (ocean)

湖 (lake)

池 (pond)

油 (oil)

汁 (soup)

Did you find it? Yes, all of the kanji above have the same part: 氵. This common part is a radical; it comes from the kanji for water 水 and indicates that the specific kanji is somehow related to water. Ocean, lake, pond, oil, and soup are all fluids. These radicals are helpful cues when learning kanji.

REMEMBER

There are variations of radicals, but we presented the one used in the kanji introduced in this book.

Positions of Radicals

The radicals are divided into seven categories, depending on the positions.

1		left (*hen*)	時、海、休
2		right (*tsukuri*)	部、頭、利
3		top (*kan'muri*)	今、学、花
4		bottom (*ashi*)	見、六、書

5		enclosure (*kamae*)	国、図
			円、聞
			医、区
6		upper left (*tare*)	病、広、原
7		lower left (*nyō*)	起、道、建

Writing Kanji

Writing kanji can be quite a pleasant experience. You concentrate on each line and draw an elegant character. When you finish drawing your favorite kanji, it can be a "wow" moment. So, I will show you a few things to keep in mind in order to produce beautiful kanji.

Stroke order

When you first encounter a kanji with many lines, you may wonder how it could possibly be written! Don't worry. There is a method for tackling this challenge. The lines in kanji are often referred to as strokes; they can be longer lines, short dot–like lines, or hooks that you use to finish lines. Here are some basic principles for stroke order that you can refer to.

Fundamental principles

Vertical strokes are written from top to bottom.

Horizontal strokes are written from left to right.

Basic stroke order

If you have both horizontal and vertical lines, write the horizontal line first.

(examples: 十, 土)

If you have a center line and sweeping lines on both sides, start with the center line and then create the left and right lines.

(examples: 小, 水)

If you don't have a center line, but there are sweeping lines on both sides, start with the left stroke.

(examples: 人, 父)

When you have enclosures, start with the outside stroke. The left vertical line comes first.

(examples: 四, 内)

If there is a vertical piercing line in the middle, draw that line last.

(examples: 中, 東)

If there is a horizontal piercing line, draw that line last.

(examples: 女, 子)

These are the basic rules for drawing kanji, but not every kanji follows them; in fact, there are more detailed rules for certain kanji. Nonetheless, these basic rules will be very helpful. The more you learn kanji, the more you will get the hang of the order of strokes. Keep practicing! Writing kanji will help you learn stroke order, and this will help you remember kanji.

REMEMBER

Each stroke is drawn with one continuous movement.

Types of strokes

There are three types of strokes that are especially important in Japanese calligraphy: *tome* (stop), *hane* (hook), and *harai* (release).

Tome

Hane

Harai

If you have a chance to use a brush and ink, I hope you try it. You will come to understand kanji even more!

REMEMBER

You can refer to this chapter while practicing kanji in the next chapter. Now it's time to grab a pencil and some extra paper and get started!

 **one**

ICHI/hito

Ichi is one of the simplest kanji to write: a single line. Although it looks easy, the old version wasn't so simple and looked like this 壱. The old kanji can still be found on the 10,000 yen bill with the portrait of Fukuzawa Yukichi, a famous nineteenth–century philosopher/educator. This kanji is used in words such as 一 日 *ichi nichi* (one day), 十 一 *jūichi*(eleven), and 一 人 *hitori* (one person, alone).

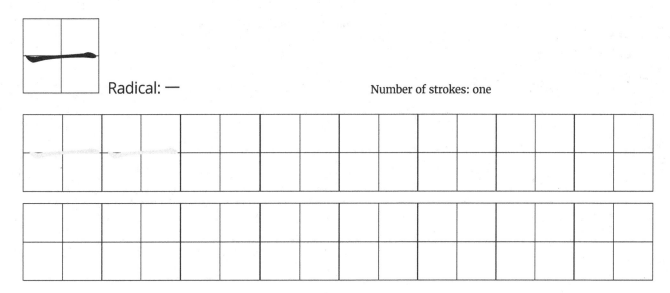

Radical: 一

Number of strokes: one

 **two**

NI/futa

Just like the number one, the kanji for "two" is extremely easy to write. Also like the number one, it's much easier to write than its "old" version, which looked like this 弐. You can still find the old style on the 2,000 yen bill. You will find this kanji in compounds like 二 月 *nigatsu* (February), 十 二 *jūni* (twelve), and 二 人 *futari* (two people).

Radical: 二

Number of strokes: two

三 . three

SAN/mi

The traditional character for the number three was 参. The modern, and simpler, version of this kanji is pronounced "mi," as in the surname of the Japanese novelist *Mi-shima* 三島
みしま
(literally three islands). It's used in words such as 三 月
さんがつ
sangatsu (March, the third month), 十 三 *jūsan* (thirteen),
じゅうさん
and 三 人 *san'nin* (three people).
さんにん

Radical: 三

Number of strokes: three

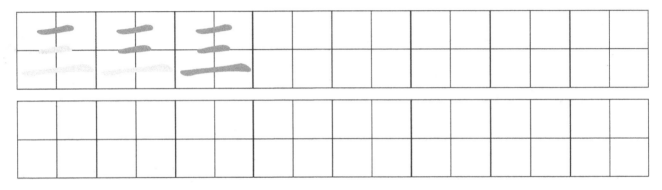

四 . four

SHI/yon

Starting from the number four, things get a little more complicated. Well, we can't draw horizontal lines forever, so four looks a bit different: 四. One thing that stands out about this kanji is its pronunciation: *shi* is homophonous with another kanji that means "death." That's why this number is not particularly liked in Japan. It's used in words such as 四月
しがつ
shigatsu (April), 十 四 *jūyon* (fourteen), and 四人 *yonin*
じゅうよん   よにん
(four people).

Radical: 口

Number of strokes: five

 **five**

GO/itsu

Go, let's "go" — you're on the right path for learning kanji! And speaking of paths, when you trace this kanji, notice that the third stroke has a corner. In general, bent or curved lines are written as one line. You can find this kanji in compounds such as 五月 *gogatsu* (May), 十五 *jūgo* (fifteen), and 五人 *gonin* (five people).

 Radical: 二   Number of strokes: four

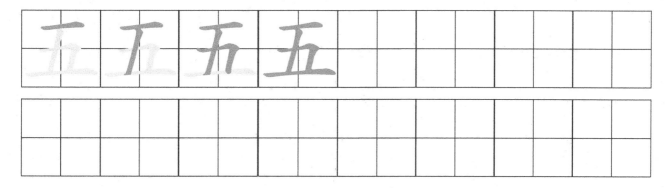

 **six**

ROKU/mu

Six rocks! *Roku* is comprised of four strokes, and is very simple to write. You can combine *roku* with other kanji to write 六月 *rokugatsu* (June), 十六 *jūroku* (sixteen), 六人 *rokunin* (six people), and more!

 Radical: 八   Number of strokes: four

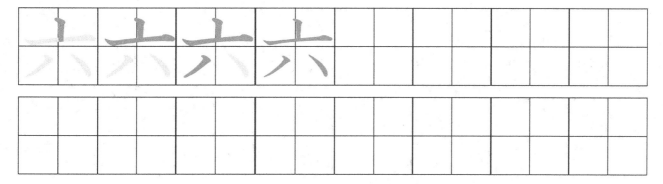

 **seven**

SHICHI/nana

Are you a big fan of Japanese samurai movies? Then you probably know the film, *Seven Samurai*. In Japanese, it's called *Shichinin no samurai*. John Sturges was so inspired by this famous Akira Kurosawa film that he created *The Magnificent Seven*. You will see this kanji in 七 人 *shichinin* (seven people), 七 月 *shichigatsu* (July, the "seventh month"), 十七 *jūnana* (seventeen), and other seven-related compounds!

 Radical: 一　　　　　　　　　　　　Number of strokes: two

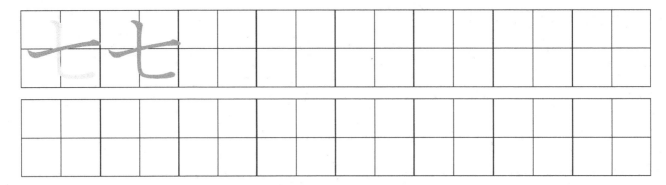

 **eight**

HACHI/ya

Hachi sounds like "hatch," but it has two syllables (beats). You can combine it with other kanji to create words such as 八 月 *hachigatsu* (August), 十 八 *jūhachi* (eighteen), and 八 人 *hachinin* (eight people).

 Radical: 八　　　　　　　　　　　　Number of strokes: two

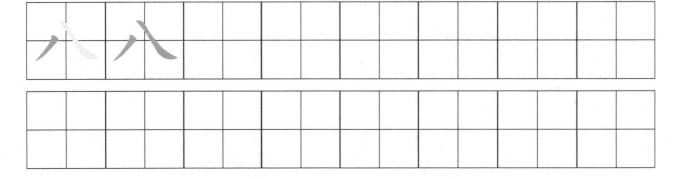

 **nine**

KYŪ, KU/kokono

This kanji is relatively simple to write. Just like the number five, 五, the line with a corner is written as a single line. 九 *kyū* is found in the name of one of the four main islands of Japan, called 九州 *Kyūshū*. This kanji is used for words related to the number nine, such as 九月 *kugatsu* (September), 十九 *jūkyū* (nineteen), and 九人 *kyūnin* (nine people).

 Radical: 乙   Number of strokes: two

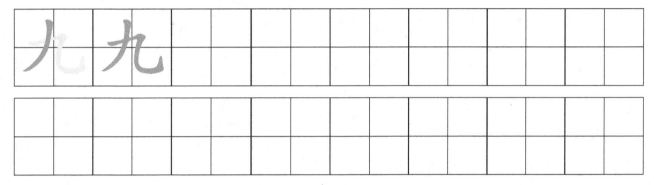

 **ten**

JŪ/tō

This is an easy kanji to memorize because it reminds you of a cross. It's no coincidence, then, that the Red Cross is called 赤十字 *sekijūji* (literally red ten character). From ten on, you can add the numbers from one to nine, to get 十一 *jūichi*, 十二 *jūni*, 十三 *jūsan*, and so on. To get the number twenty, you place the numbers two and ten consecutively: 二十 *nijū*. By applying this system, you are able to write up to 99. You can also use this kanji to write the last three months of the year: 十月 *jūgatsu* (October), 十一月 *jūichigatsu* (November), and 十二月 *jūnigatsu* (December). Easy enough, isn't it?

 Radical: 十   Number of strokes: two

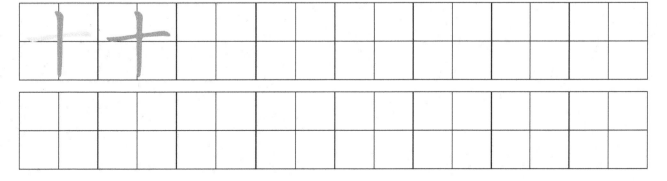

hundred

百 **HYAKU/momo**

From the hundred 百 *hyaku*, we can continue to count: 百　一 *hyaku ichi* (101), 百　二 ひゃくいち ／ ひゃくに *hyakuni* (102), 百三 *hyakusan* (103), and so on. To obtain the hundreds, you can write 二　百 にひゃく *nihyaku*, 三　百 *sanbyaku*, 四　百 *yonhyaku*, 五　百 *gohyaku*, 六　百 *roppyaku*, 七　百 さんびゃく ／ よんひゃく ／ ごひゃく ／ ろっぴゃく ／ ななひゃく *nanahyaku*, 八　百 *happyaku*, 九　百 *kyūhyaku*. Note that the sound of *hyaku* changes はっぴゃく ／ きゅうひゃく according to the kanji that precedes one hundred. *Hyaku* can be combined with other kanji, such as 百　円 *hyaku.en* (one hundred yen) or 百　人 *hyakunin* (one hundred people). ひゃくえん ／ ひゃくにん

Radical: 百　　　　　　　　　　Number of strokes: six

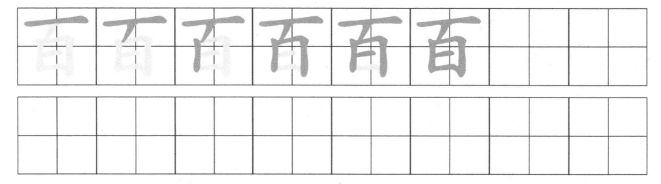

thousand

千 **SEN/chi**

From *sen*, we can continue to count *sen.ichi* (1,001), *sen.ni* (1,002), *sen.san* (1,003), and so on. You write thousands as 二　千 *nisen* (two thousand), 三　千 *sanzen* (three thousand), 四　千 *yonsen* にせん ／ さんぜん ／ よんせん (four thousand), 五　千 *gosen* (five thousand), 六　千 *rokusen* (six thousand), 七　千 *nanasen* ごせん ／ ろくせん ／ ななせん (seven thousand), 八　千 *hassen* (eight thousand), 九　千 *kyūsen* (nine thousand). The year はっせん ／ きゅうせん 2019, the beginning of the new era called *Reiwa* will be 二千十九 *nisenjūkyū-nen* with *nen* being the counter for years. You can also combine the numbers with other counters. For example, you can add *nin*, the counter for people, to *sen* to say 千　人 *sennin*, which means "1,000 people." せんにん

Radical: 千　　　　　　　　　　Number of strokes: three

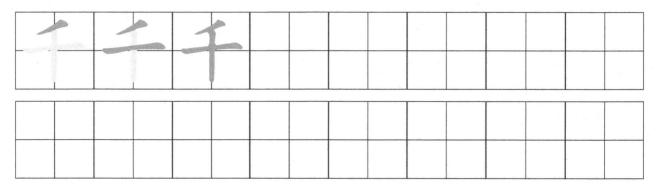

ten thousand

MAN, BAN/
yorozu

In Japanese, "ten thousand" is a unit and has its own kanji, 万 *man*, which indicates the number of 10,000s. The old writing of this kanji is 萬, and it is used on the Japanese 10,000 yen bill. You need to add 一 *ichi* to indicate the number "10,000," and so it becomes 一万 いちまん *ichiman* (unlike 100 *hyaku*, and 1,000 *sen*, which can stand on their own). To indicate a number of 10,000s, you place a number before *man*, as in 二万 にまん *niman* (20,000) and 五万 ごまん *goman* (50,000). To talk about Japanese currency, you can combine *man* with 円 えん *en* to create 一万円 いちまんえん *ichiman.en* (ten thousand yen). In general, Arabic numerals are commonly used to show numbers in Japan, but kanji is also used in many places.

Radical: 一   Number of strokes: three

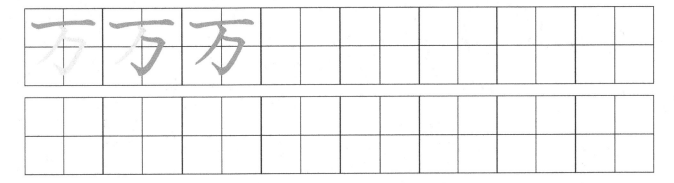

person, people

NIN, JIN/
hito

The basic meaning of this kanji is *person* or *people*; in fact, by looking at it, you can imagine a person walking. However, *jin* is also used to refer to nationalities. You do this by combining the country and 人 じん *jin*, as in *supeinjin* (Spaniard; literally Spain people/person), *amerikajin* (American; literally America people/person), *roshiajin* (Russian; literally Russia people/person), *furansujin* (Frenchmen/man; literally France people/person), *itariajin* (Italian; literally Italy people/person), and so on. The term for Japanese people/person is *nihonjin*, which is a combination of *Nihon* (Japan) and *jin*. To talk about a person, or people in general, we say *hito* 人. If you have a lover, we say 恋人 こいびと *koibito*.

Radical: 人   Number of strokes: two

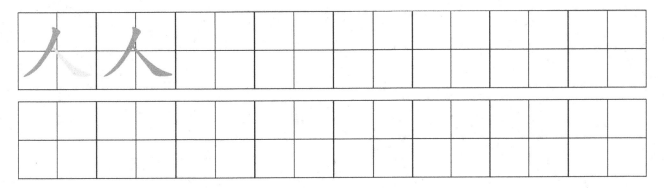

CHAPTER 3 105 Characters   **27**

woman, female

On'na is a generic term for a woman. 女の子 on'na no ko is a small or young girl. 女性 josei is a more formal term for a woman (literally, female gender). You can use on'na by itself, but this word is often used to indicate the actual gender and thus is not really appropriate when referring to a woman. When you write this kanji, make sure to start with the curved line from the top, not the horizontal line. And when you draw the curved line, aim for a 90-degree angle at the left corner.

JO, NYO/
on'na

Radical: 女   Number of strokes: three

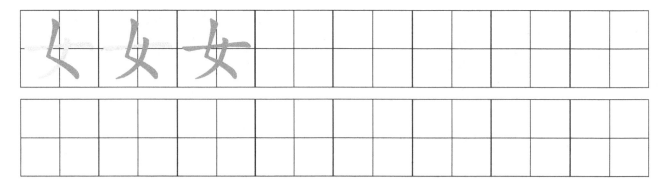

man/male

Does this kanji look complicated? No worries! It does have seven strokes, but if you learn each constituent in a systematic manner, you will find this kanji to be quite simple. The stroke order of this kanji starts from the left vertical line in the box-like part. Take a look at the stroke order in the practice section below; if you follow the drawing order shown here, the movement will come naturally afterwards. Otoko is a general term that means a man. 男の子 otoko no ko means a small or young boy. 男性 dansei is a more formal term for a man (literally male gender). Just like on'na, you can use otoko by itself, but in regular conversation, it sounds somewhat impolite. So, stick with dansei or otoko no hito.

DAN/otoko

Radical: 田   Number of strokes: seven

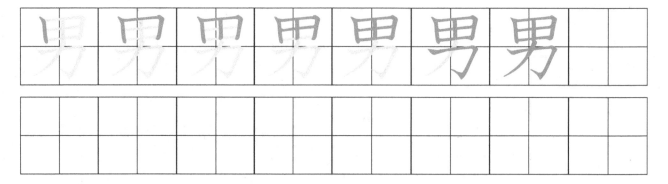

mouth

This kanji looks like a square. You might think it's not really like a mouth, but imagine rounded lips being stylized into a square. It also designates a passage. For example, this kanji is used for compound words such as 出口 *deguchi* (exit) and 入口 *iriguchi* (entrance). Note that it is drawn with three lines, not four. The second stroke starts from the top left, goes horizontally to the right, makes a sharp turn in the top-right corner, and then goes down to the bottom.

KOU, KU/
kuchi

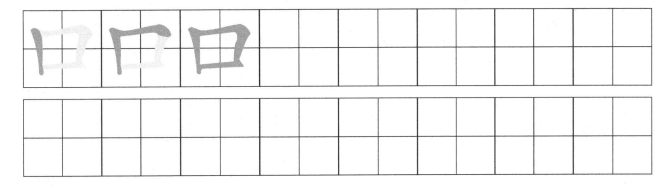

Radical: 口   Number of strokes: three

eye

MOKU, BOKU/
me

Originally this kanji probably looked like an eye with a pupil in its center. The two central horizontal lines still show that basic shape. The pictograph that showed an eye became more abstract, but with a little imagination, you can see an eye. You can

combine this kanji with others to create words such as 一目 *hitome* (glance) and
目的 *mokuteki* (goal or purpose).

Radical: 目   Number of strokes: five

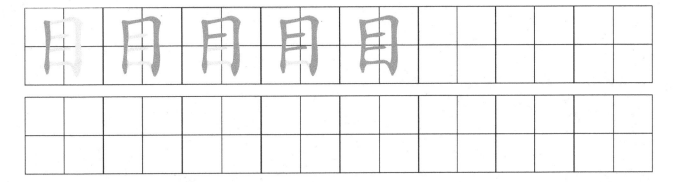

 **ear**

JI/mimi

You probably noticed that this kanji looks like the previous kanji, *me* (eye), except that the vertical and horizontal lines are a little longer. A great observation! You just have to pull the 'ears' by extending the lines. The following phrase containing *mimi* may amuse you: *watashi wa mimi ga tōi* 私 は 耳 が 遠 い (literally the ear is far away). No worries, though! It doesn't actually mean my ear is far away! We use this expression to say that one has a little hearing problem.

 Radical: 耳   Number of strokes: six

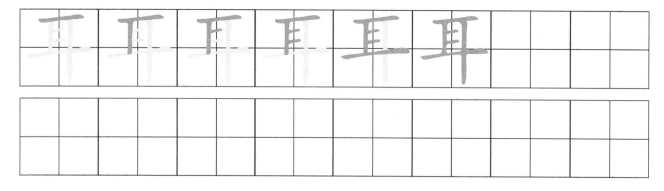

 **hand**

SHU/te

This kanji may not look like a hand, but let's imagine fingers. 手*te* means "hand" by itself. In winter, you wear gloves, 手 袋 *tebukuro*. Literally, this means "hand-bag" — bags for hands! Other examples are 手 紙 *tegami* (letter) and 切 手 *kitte* (stamp). A professional singer is 歌手*kashu*.

 Radical: 手   Number of strokes: four

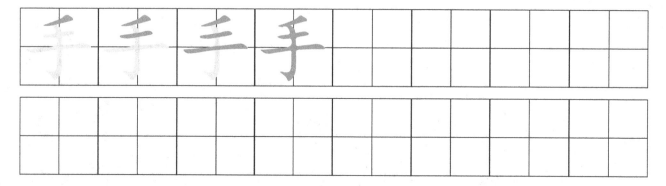

heart, mind

心

SHIN/kokoro

Kokoro is a complex word. It means heart, soul, spirit, or the essence of something. It does
not imply the actual organ; for that, you would use 心臓 *shinzō*, which is a kanji compound word that literally means "heart organ." *Kokoro* is an important kanji that is fre-
quently evoked in classical poetry. There are many expressions with *kokoro*. For example,
心が広い *kokoro ga hiroi*, which literally means "the heart is wide," refers to someone
who is generous and broad-minded.

Radical: 心　　　　　　　　　　　　　　　　Number of strokes: four

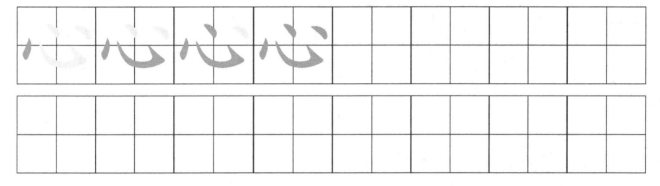

up, above, top

上

JŌ, SHŌ/ue,
a(garu), nobo(ru)

This kanji is used to show what is above or superior. For example, 机の上 *tsukue no
ue*, literally means "on top of the desk," so, above the desk. It also extends the meaning to "high." The compound word 上級 *jōkyū* means "advanced level." 上手
jōzu means "good at (something)." It can also mean "climb" or "ascend." 上がる *agaru*
means "to go up," and 上る *noboru* means "to climb." When you see this kanji, you
can guess it's about something upward. In Japanese, the words that indicate spatial
relationships, such as top, bottom, inside, and so on, are typically nouns.

Radical: 一　　　　　　　　　　　　　　　　Number of strokes: three

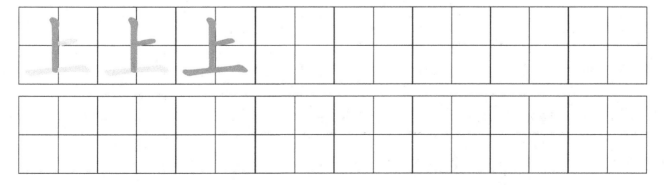

under, below, bottom

GE, KA/shita,
sa(garu), o(riru)

Shita is the opposite of the previous kanji. It means "below" and "inferior" as in
机 の 下 *tsukue no shita* (under the desk) and 部下 *buka* (subordinates). Just like 上
ue, 下 *shita* is a noun. However, when it's pronounced 下りる *oriru*, it means "to go
down." The other pronunciation, 下がる *sagaru*, means "to descend."

Radical: 一

Number of strokes: three

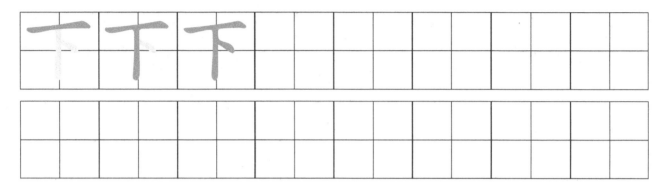

before, previous, front

ZEN/mae

This kanji designates what is before you or what comes before, from a temporal or spatial point of view. For example, 机 の 前 *tsuke no mae* means "in front of the desk."

When it's combined with the kanji 日 (day), it becomes 前 日 *zenjitsu* (the day before).

By adding the kanji meaning "name" in front of 前, you can make the compound 名前
namae, which means "name." When you fill out any kind of official documents, you'll
see this word!

Radical: 刂

Number of strokes: nine

after, behind

GO, KŌ/ato,
nochi, ushi(ro)

Radical: 彳

This kanji is a bit more complicated to write as it has nine lines. It can be used to locate an object or a place, or to specify the moment of an action in time. 後ろ *ushiro* means "behind" to point out the location of someone or something, whereas 後 *ato* means "after" or "later." For example, 机 の 後 ろ *tsukue no ushiro* is "behind the desk." When you want to say, "See you later," you can say じゃ、また 後 で *Ja mata atode.*

Numbers of strokes: nine

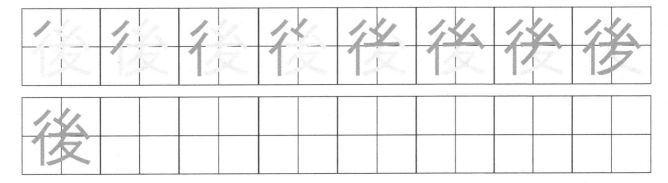

outside

GAI/soto

外 *soto* refers to what is outside or what is foreign. *Soto* is always a noun unlike "outside" in English. For example, "outside the house" is 家の外 *ie no soto*, although "outside" in this English phrase is a preposition. It is also found in compounds like 外 国 *gaikoku* (foreign country) and 外 見 *gaiken* (external appearance, or simply, appearance). When you add 人 (person/people) to 外 国, the compound word becomes 外 国 人 *gaikokujin*, (foreigners). Note that the word 外 人 *gaijin* is avoided in polite conversation.

Radical: 夕

Number of strokes: five

inside

 NAI/uchi

The word *uchi* refers to everything inside, to a circle of people, to a space, or to a community. When you learn Japanese culture, you may hear the concept of *uchi* and *soto*. For example, your family members are considered *uchi*, but your colleagues are people from *soto*. However, if you are in the workplace, your colleagues are people associated with *uchi*. Yes, it is a

bit complicated. You may see this kanji in expressions such as 内 の子 *uchi no ko* (my child) and 内 容 *naiyō* (content).

Radical: 冂 Number of strokes: four

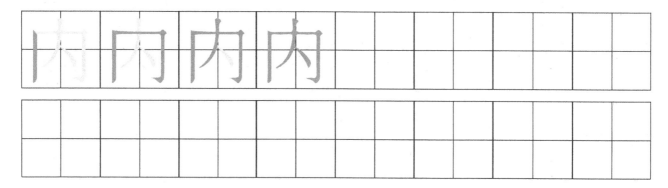

middle, center, inside

 **CHŪ/naka**

This kanji is very simple to create and easy to remember. As shown here, you draw a flattened box and a long line in the middle. Remember, you should draw the left vertical line of the box first. かばんの 中 *kaban no naka* means "inside the bag" and 中 国 *Chūgoku* is

China, the middle country. Combining this kanji with the kanji for "heart," you get 中 心 *chūshin* (central, in the center).

Radical: 丨 Number of strokes: four

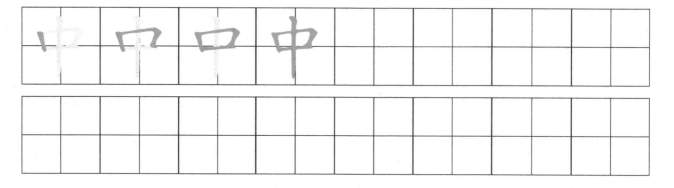

北 . north

HOKU/kita

We find this kanji in many family names, such as 北川 *kitagawa* きたがわ
and 北野 *kitano*. きたの When you travel by train, you will notice that the larger stations have more than one exit or entrance; the north exit or entrance is called 北口 *kitaguchi*. きたぐち You can also find this kanji in the name of a region of Japan called 東北 *Tōhoku*. とうほく The Tōhoku region comprises the northern part of the largest island, named Honshu. This region is known for its beautiful landscapes in autumn, when the leaves of the trees change color.

Radical: 匕

Number of strokes: five

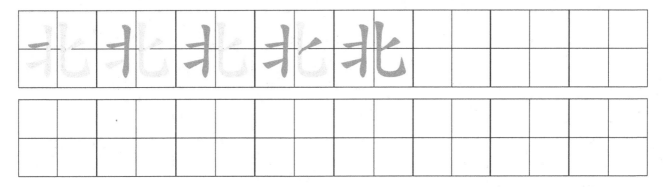

西 . west

SAI, SEI/nishi

This kanji refers to the west, and to all that is to the west. It appears in a common phrase, 西も東もわからない *nishi mo higashi mo wakaranai* にし ひがし (someone who has no idea about something or about directions). Just like 北 *kita* (north), きた you may see 西口 *nishiguchi* にしぐち (west exit or entrance) at a train station. 西 *sei* also means "western" or "European." For example, 西洋 *seiyō* せいよう can mean both Europe and America.

Radical: 西

Number of strokes: six

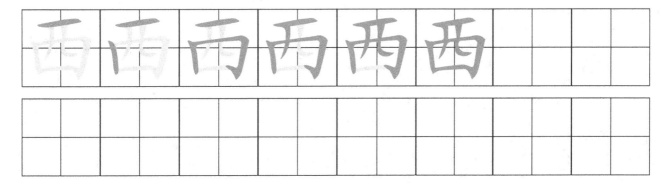

南 . south

NAN/minami

This kanji means "south." For example, 南 アメリカ *Minami Amerika* is South America. 南下 *nanka* means "to go south," although this doesn't imply something bad! 南部 *nanbu* refers to a southern part of a region.

Radical: 十

Number of strokes: nine

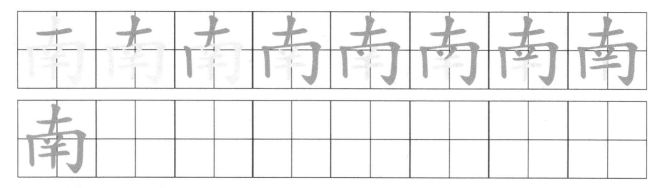

東 . east

TŌ/higashi

Japan is an archipelago located east of China, but west of the United States. It all depends on your geographical point of view. For a long time, Kyoto was Japan's capital, but after the Meiji Restoration, the new Japanese government settled in the city of Edo, which was renamed 東京 *Tōkyō*, the capital of the East. At a train station (yes, you guessed it!), you may see a sign labeled 東口 *higashi-guchi* (east exit or entrance).

Radical: 木

Number of strokes: eight

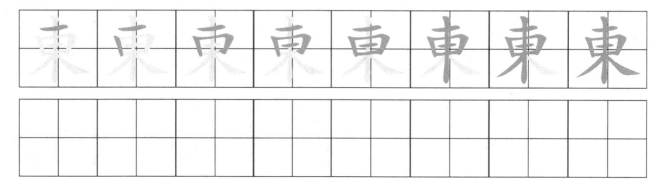

日 • sun, day

NICHI, JITSU/hi

にほん
You will find this kanji in 日本 *Nihon* or *Nippon* (Japan), which is somewhat poetically translated in the West as the Land of the Rising Sun. It should not be confused with the kanji for "fire," which has the same pronunciation, *hi*. You can use this kanji to refer to days of the week. For example, 日よう日 *nichiyōbi* is "Sunday." (As you will have noticed here, you can use the same kanji twice in a word when it's appropriate!)

Radical: 日

Number of strokes: four

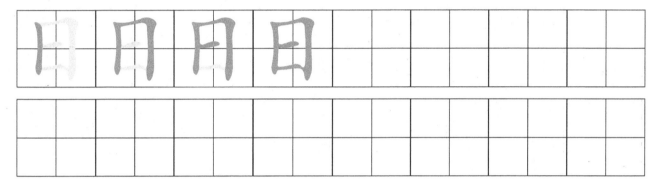

月 • moon

GATSU, GETSU/

tsuki

Like cherry blossoms, the moon is a very important element in both traditional and popular Japanese culture. Japanese people especially appreciate the full moon in autumn. Viewing of the moon is called
つきみ
月見 *tsukimi*. This kanji is also used to indicate months and days of the week, such as 一月 *ichigatsu* (January) and 月よう日 *getsuyōbi* (Monday).

Radical: 月

Number of strokes: four

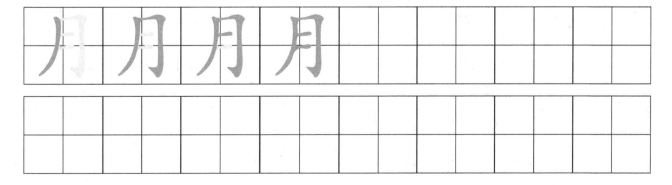

DO/tsuchi

soil, earth

This is a relatively simple kanji to write. It is found in compounds such as 土よう日 *doyōbi* (Saturday) and 土台 *dodai* (foundation or base).

Radical: 土

Number of strokes: three

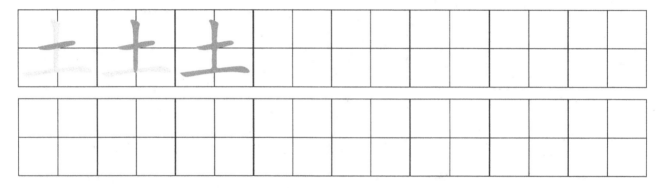

KA/hi

fire

Does this kanji evoke a campfire flame? It looks like fire dancing, doesn't it? If you add the kanji for "flower" before this kanji, it becomes 花火 *hanbi* (fireworks). If you add "flower" *after* this kanji, you get 火花 *hibana* (spark). If you add the kanji for "mouth," you get 火口 *kakō* (crater). This kanji is also used in 火よう日 *kayōbi* (Tuesday).

Radical: 火

Number of strokes: four

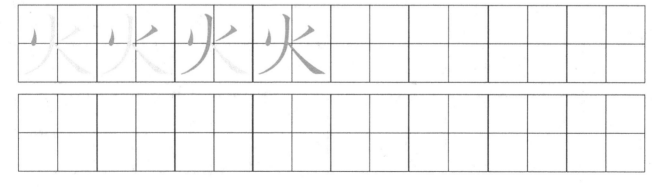

SUI/mizu

water

When you see this kanji, you can assume that the word is related to water. *Mizu* simply means "water." When we ask for water, we often say お水 *omizu* (water). There are many compound words with this kanji. For example, a light blue may be described with 水色 *mizuiro* (literally color of water). When it's combined with the kanji for "ball," it becomes 水玉 *mizutama* (literally water ball), which means "polka dot." When you cook, your recipe may say 水煮する *mizuni'suru* (boil in water). This kanji is also found in 水よう日 *suiyōbi* (Wednesday).

Radical: 水

Number of strokes: four

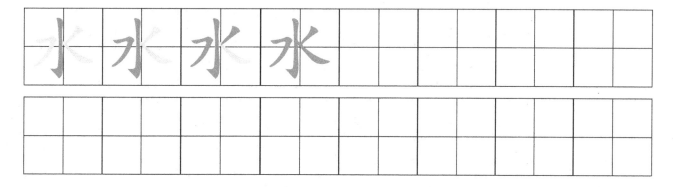

wind

FŪ, PU/kaze

When you say *kaze*, it simply means "wind." You can enjoy a pleasant breeze, そよ風 *soyo-kaze*, in early summer. But Japan is regularly hit by natural disasters, such as 台風 *taifū* (typhoons). As a result, the archipelago is swept by high winds described as 強風 *kyōfū*.

This kanji also indicates manners or styles. For example, 風習 *fūshū* means customs practiced in a society.

Radical: 風

Number of strokes: nine

 mountain

SAN/yama

Can you imagine a mountain summit looking at this kanji? The most famous Japanese mountain is, of course, Mt. Fuji, which is called in Japan 富士山 ふじさん *Fujisan* (not Fujiyama). Japan is a mountainous country, so you see this kanji used to form family names, location names, names of trees, and so on. Using the kanji for fire, 火, you can make "volcano," which is 火山 かざん *kazan*. Note that *san* is pronounced as *zan* in some kanji compounds.

 Radical: 山

Number of strokes: three

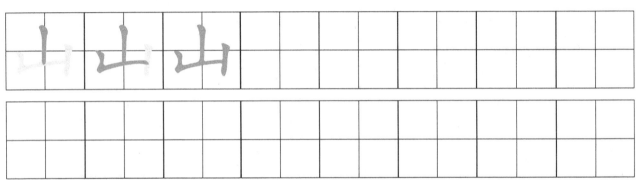

 river

SEN/kawa

Like the kanji for "mountain," the kanji for "river" is undoubtedly one of the most faithful in its form to the ancient writing. These three lines are easy to memorize. When you write this kanji, you are reproducing a peaceful flow of water. The longest river in Japan is しなのがわ 信濃川 *Shinanogawa*. You probably noticed something here: yes, *kawa* becomes *gawa* in some kanji compounds. This kanji is also found in family names or local names, as in the city of 川崎 かわさき *Kawasaki*.

Radical: 川

Number of strokes: three

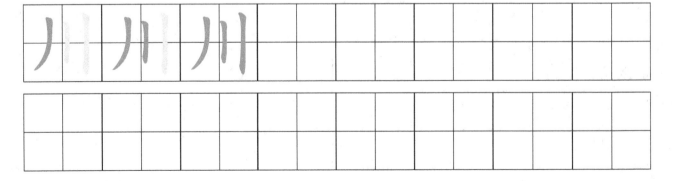

ocean, sea

KAI/umi

Remember this kanji! Because Japan is made up of islands surrounded by water, you will see it a lot in Japan. For example, 海岸 *kaigan* (かいがん) means "seashore." We also find it in 海外 *kaigai* (かいがい), meaning "overseas." When you say *umi*, that's "ocean."

Radical: 氵 (This radical is used with water-related kanji.)　　　Number of strokes: nine

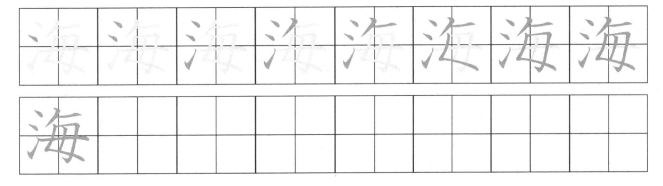

rice field

DEN/ta

Rice is a staple food in Japan, so you can see rice fields in many agricultural areas. Rice fields are also called rice paddies in English due to their water-filled fields. There are narrow pathways around the rice paddies, as shown in this kanji; you can also just imagine a small checkerboard to help memorize it. This kanji is found in many Japanese surnames, such as 田中 (たなか) *Tanaka*.

Radical: 田　　　　　Number of strokes: five

 **tree**

BOKU, MOKU/
ki, ko

When you say *ki*, it means "tree." When you see this kanji in a compound word, you can guess that the word is somehow related to trees. For example, 木目 *mokume* means "wood grain." 神 木 *shinboku* (literally god tree) is a tree that is typically found in a Shinto shrine and is considered sacred. This kanji is also used for 木 よう日 *mokuyōbi* (Thursday).

 Radical: 木

Number of strokes: four

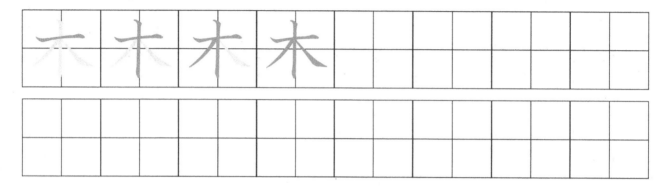

 **now**

KON,KIN/ima

When you say *ima*, that means "now." A useful sentence, 今、何時です か。*Ima nanji desu ka*, means "What time is it now?" When you write this kanji, you start from the top of the kanji and draw two nice, flowing lines, first to the left, and then to the right. The combination of the two kanji, "now" 今 and "day" 日, gives two new words, with different pronunciations and meanings. 今日*Kyō* is "today" but 今日*konnichi* is "nowadays." And 今日は*kon'nichiwa* is "hello."

 Radical: 人

Number of strokes: four

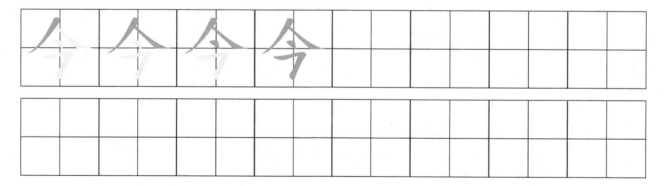

朝 · morning

CHŌ/asa

朝 Radical: 月

Things seem to get complicated with this kanji, because we suddenly go to twelve strokes. But no worries, you already know each constituent. Let's first look at the left side: do you see 十、日, and 十 in a vertical arrangement? Now check out the right side: it's the kanji for "moon." So, you have ten, sun, ten, and moon. You will see this kanji in one of the most respected newspapers in Japan, called 朝 日 新 聞 *Asahi shimbun*.

Number of strokes: twelve

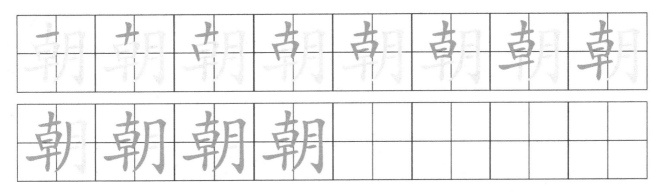

夜 · night

YA/yo,

yoru

夜 Radical: 夕

Yoru has its own charm. The combination of "moon" and "night" makes a poetic 月 夜 *tsukiyo* (moon-lit night). "Tonight" is 今 夜 *kon'ya*, which is the combination of 今 (now) and 夜 (night).

Number of strokes: eight

犬 · dog

KEN/inu

Man's best friend looks like this in kanji. Strange? It may not look like a dog to you. Note that it looks very much like the kanji for 大 (big); but a little dot in its upper-right corner makes "big" a dog. You will find this kanji in あきたいぬ
秋田犬 *akitainu* (Akita dog), which is the breed of the famous Hachi, the dog who waited for his owner at the train station every day, not knowing the owner had passed away. Do you have an *inu* as a pet?

 Radical: 犬   Number of strokes: four

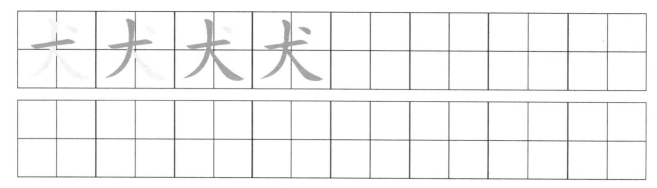

猫 · cat

BYŌ/neko

The left part of this kanji indicates that the character refers to something about animals, although the kanji for "dog" does not have this part. Perhaps dogs are more domesticated than cats? But a cat is an auspicious animal for businesses. Have you seen a little cat figure beckoning with its paw in a shop まね　ねこ
or restaurant? These cat figures are called 招き猫 *maneki-neko*. They nod to you to welcome you and invite fortune for their owners!

 Radical: 犭   Number of strokes: eleven

cow, cattle

A cow is not a sacred animal in Japan. Nevertheless, the Japanese consider eating it a "sacred" experience, as Kobe beef is good "melting meat," and one of the best in the world! Thus, the

Japanese eat not only sushi, but also grilled or stewed 牛 *ushi*. Beef bowls called 牛丼 <ruby>牛丼<rt>ぎゅうどん</rt></ruby> *gyūdon* are very popular as well.

GYŪ/ushi

Radical: 牛   Number of strokes: four

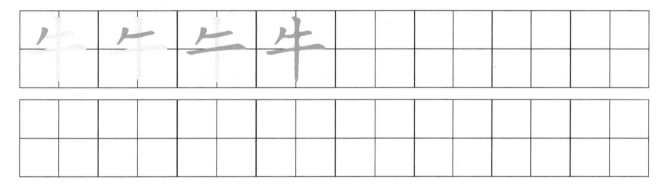

fish

Japan is known for its cuisine based on raw fish, such as sushi and sashimi. But fish are also grilled there, and you can find grilled mackerel, salmon, saber-fish, and so on. The combi-

nation of 金 (gold) and 魚 (fish) makes 金魚 <ruby>金魚<rt>きんぎょ</rt></ruby> *kingyo* (gold fish). There are also decorative fish — carp, or *koi* — swimming in basins, and you can even find them floating in the wind. The floating *koi* is called *koinobori,* which celebrates "Children's Day." But these are made of fabric or paper, so they're not for your empty stomach!

GYO/sakana, uo

Radical: 魚   Number of strokes: eleven

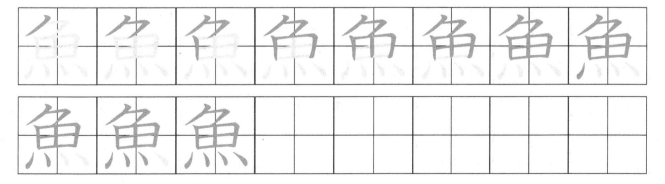

肉 . meat

NIKU

When you go grocery shopping in Japan, you can find this kanji on the labels in the meat section. If you can add this kanji to the kanji for cow, pork, or chicken, you can make compounds like 牛 肉 gyūniku (beef), 豚 肉 butaniku (pork), and 鳥 肉 toriniku (chicken). Are you an athlete? If so, then you must have strong 筋 肉 kin.niku (muscles).

Radical: 肉   Number of strokes: six

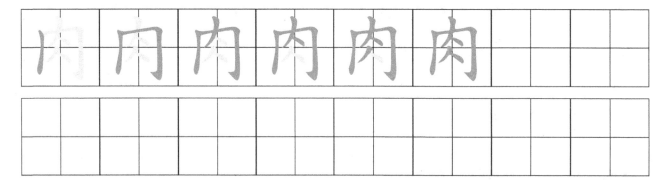

花 . flower

KA/hana

The word hana (flower) has a special place in Japanese culture. Flowers are often described in Japanese literature, especially in traditional poetry. In springtime, Japanese people enjoy viewing *sakura*, cherry blossoms, which are admired as a symbol of elegant and ephemeral beauty. This can be combined with the kanji for "fire" to create the combination for 花火 *hanabi* (fireworks); *hanabi* often accompany summer festivals.

Radical: 艹   Number of strokes: seven

母 · mother

BO/haha

There are different ways to say "mother," which can make your life a little complicated. When you talk about your own mother with someone who is not that close to you, say your boss at work, you refer to her as 母 *haha*. When you talk to someone about their mother, you say お母さん *okāsan*. When you call your own mother at home, you may say お母さん *okāsan* as well. Your grandmother is 祖母 *sobo*.

 Radical: 母

Number of strokes: five

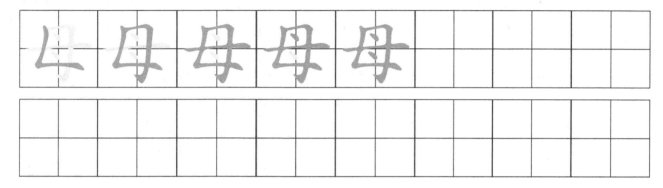

父 · father

FU/chichi

お父さん *otōsan* is a respectful term for "father." Just like "mother," when you are talking about someone else's father, you may say お父さん *otōsan*, but when you refer to your own father, you should say 父 *chichi*. Within your household, you might call your own father *otōsan* and your grandfather 祖父 *sofu*.

 Radical: 父

Number of strokes: four

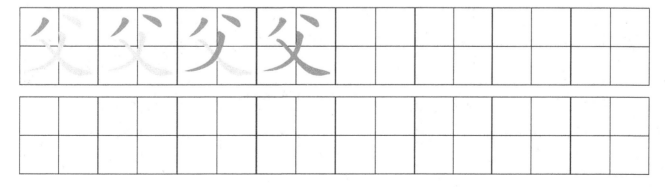

older brother

Just like the kanji for "father" and "mother," this kanji is used to refer to one's "older brother," but there are different ways of saying it. When you are talking about someone else's older brother, you may say お兄さん *onīsan*. This word also refers to young men. But when you refer to your own older brother, you should say 兄 *ani*. Within the household, you might call your own brother お兄ちゃん *onīchan*. *Chan* is a diminutive.

Radical: 儿   Number of strokes: five

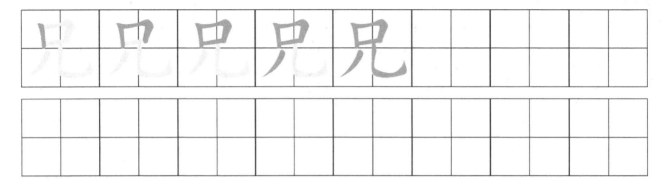

older sister

As you might have guessed, this kanji also follows the rules that are presented for "father," "mother," and "brother"! お姉さん*onēsan* refers respectfully to a big sister. Just like *onīsan*, it can also indicate a young woman. When you talk about your big sister to someone who is not a member of your family, you should say 姉*ane*. The radical on the left of this kanji means "woman" and appears in many kanji related to women.

Radical: 女   Number of strokes: eight

younger brother

DAI, DE, TEI/
otōto

Do you have siblings? When you combine this kanji with the kanji for "older brother," you create the combination 兄 弟 *kyōdai*, which means "siblings." When you refer to your own little brother when speaking to a non-family member, it's *otōto*, but when you refer to someone else's younger brother, you should say 弟 さん *otōto-san*, using the respectful term *san*. You might have heard about the tradition of apprenticeship in art and craftsmanship in Japan. An apprentice is called 弟子 *deshi*.

Radical: 弓   Number of strokes: seven

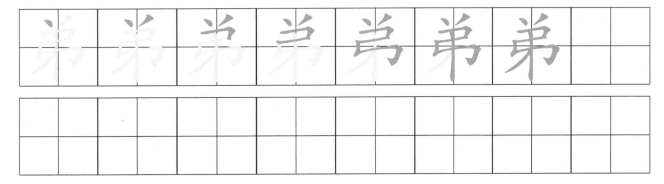

child

SHI, SU/ko

Does this kanji look like a little child? Perhaps like this 子? The general word for "child/children" is 子ども *kodomo*. If you see this kanji at the end of a first name such as Hiroko, Kimiko, Yōko, and such, the person is very likely a woman. Nowadays, however, there are many beautiful, creative names that do not have 子. You may see the kanji combinations, 女子 *joshi* (girls and women) and 男子 *danshi* (boys and men) in public restrooms or locker rooms in *onsen*, hot springs.

Radical: 子   Number of strokes: three

friend

"Friend" is such an important word in many people's lives. 友 だち *tomodachi* may be one

of the first words you encounter when learning Japanese. You can also say 友 人 *yūjin* by adding 人 (person), which sounds a little more formal and adult-like. When you write this kanji, remember to start from the horizontal line.

YŪ/tomo

Radical: 又   Number of strokes: four

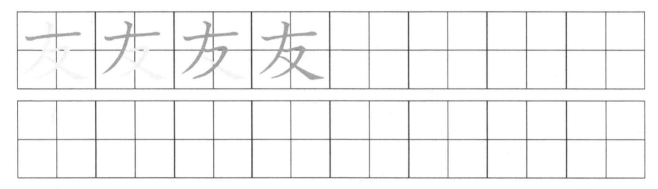

high, expensive

This kanji has a double meaning in Japanese when pronounced *takai*. 高 い *takai* means "high" or "expensive," depending on the context. Let's imagine that a two-story building

or a tower forms this kanji. Combined with another kanji, it is pronounced *kō*, as in 高 山 *kōzan* (high-altitude mountain).

KŌ/taka(i)

Radical: 高   Number of strokes: ten

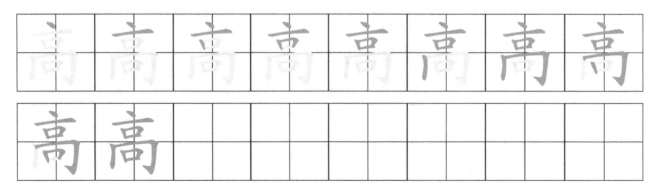

大 . big

DAI, TAI/ō(kii)

This three-line kanji is relatively easy to memorize. On the other hand, you should not confuse it with the kanji for "dog" 犬 *inu*, which has an extra dot in the upper-right corner, as you can see. 大 きい *ōkii* means "big." If you combine this kanji with another kanji, the pronunciation often becomes *dai* or *tai* as in 大 学 *daigaku* (college, university) and 大 切 *taisetsu* (something important). There are special cases like the word 大雨 *ōame* (heavy rain), which you might experience during typhoon season. When you write this kanji, remember to start from the horizontal line.

 Radical: 大

Number of strokes: three

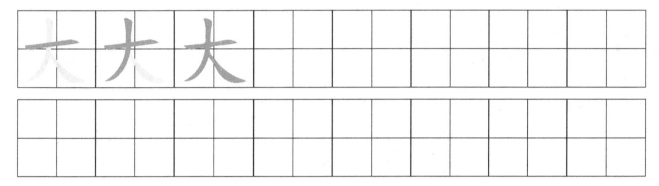

小 . small

SHŌ/chī(sai), o, ko

The adjective for "small" is 小 さい *chīsai*. When it's used in kanji compounds, it is pronounced *shō*. For example, elementary school children are called 小 学 生 *shōgakusē* (literally small students). There are other pronunciations, such as in 小石 *koishi* (small rock, pebble) and 小 川 *ogawa* (creek, brook). When you practice drawing this kanji, you start from the middle vertical line.

 Radical: 小

Number of strokes: three

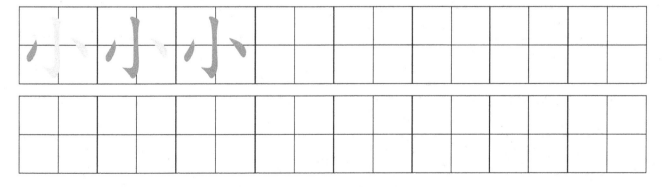

round, yen

EN/maru(i)

When you go shopping or dine out in Japan, you will encounter this kanji everywhere. It is the kanji for the Japanese currency, yen, but it is pronounced *en*. You see this kanji in Japanese banknotes and coins. When the yen becomes strong, we say it's 円 高 <ruby>円<rt>えんだか</rt></ruby> *endaka*, which literally means "expensive yen." It also means "round," which is pronounced 円い <ruby>円<rt>まる</rt></ruby> *marui*.

Radical: 冂   Number of strokes: four

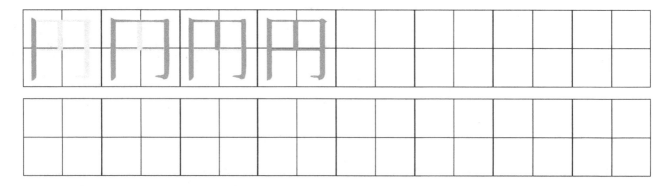

near

KIN/chika(i)

近い *chikai* is an adjective for "near." The word 近づく *chikazuku* refers to "getting closer." When you use this kanji in compounds such as 近 所 *kinjo* (neighbors and neighborhood), it is pronounced *kin*. Note that the radical is simplified in its printed version. When you practice this kanji, follow the writing model very closely, and start from the right side.

Radical: 辶   Number of strokes: seven

遠 · far

EN/tō(i)

This kanji may look very complicated due to its many small lines, so let's take a look at each of its constituents. It can be broken down into three parts: the radical is on the left, the upper part of the lines is a small version of the kanji for "earth," and the rest is the shape of a square (mouth) with four short lines on the lower part. 遠い *tōi* is an adjective that means "far" or "far in space or time." When you write this kanji, you start from 土 on the right.

Radical: ⻌   Number of strokes: thirteen

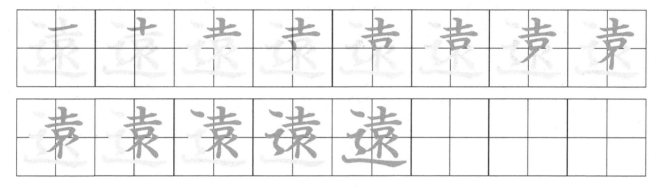

行 · to go

KŌ,GYŌ/i(ku)

This kanji means "to go" or "to go somewhere." 行く *iku* is a verb, and when it's combined with the kanji for "travel," 旅, it becomes 旅行 *ryokō* (trip, traveling), which means "going on a trip."

Radical: 行   Number of strokes: six

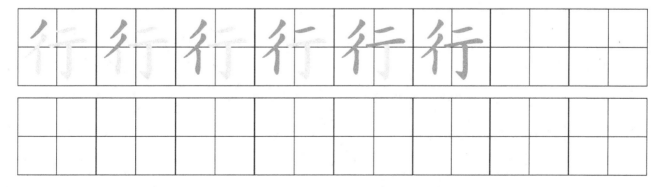

KEN/mi(ru)

to look, see

Are you wondering if you have seen this kanji before? If so, that's no surprise! Let's look at the upper part of this kanji. It looks like an eye, doesn't it? 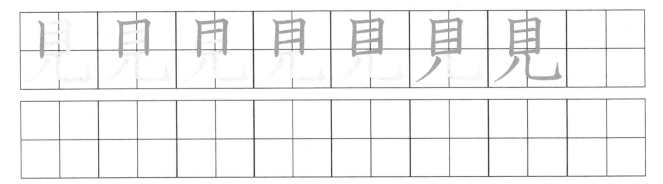Let's put legs underneath. This is the verb 見る miru, which means "look, see." Other variations include 見せる miseru (to show) and 見える mieru (to be seen). If you combine this kanji with the kanji for "one," you can make 一見 ikken (apparently; a glance).

Radical: 見

Number of strokes: seven

gate

MON/kado

This kanji resembles two saloon doors that swing open when a cowboy comes in for a drink. Well, there are no saloons in Japan, but I hope this helps you memorize this kanji. If you have seen a picture of a temple in Japan, then you may also be able to recognize the gate in this kanji. If you combine this kanji with 山 (mountain), it becomes 山門 san'mon, which refers to the main gate of a temple.

Radical: 門

Number of strokes: eight

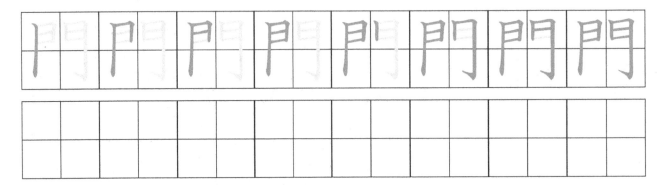

MON, BUN/
ki(ku)

to listen, hear

Did you notice that there is a gate 門 in this kanji? Under the gate, there is an ear 耳. This

kanji produces verbs such as 聞く *kiku* (listen or ask) and 聞こえる *kikoeru* (can hear).
き   き

Combined with the kanji meaning "new," we get the word 新聞 *shimbun* (newspaper), which literally means "newly hear." Makes sense, doesn't it?

 Radical: 耳

Number of strokes: fourteen

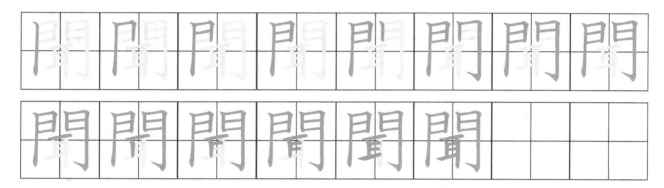

to say

言う *iu* (pronounced? *yū*) is the verb for "say." If you place a quotation mark right before the
い
verb, you can quote what someone said. For example, "(someone) says that. . ." becomes
い
"‑‑‑と 言っています" *to itteimasu*. This kanji is used as a radical in other characters such as 語 (language), 話 (story, talk), 読 (read), and many more. When you see this kanji as a part of another kanji, you can assume the character is somehow related to saying or language.

GEN, GON/i(u)

 Radical: 言

Number of strokes: seven

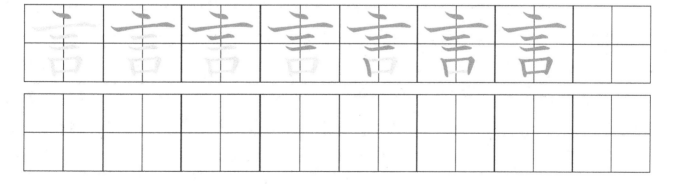

 **to buy**

BAI/ka(u)

The lower part of this kanji is the character for shell 貝 *kai*. For a long time, people used shells as money, especially in China. Today, we cannot use shells for 買い 物 *kaimono* (shopping), but Japanese people do enjoy eating shellfish. 買う *kau* is a basic verb for "buy."

 Radical: 貝   Number of strokes: twelve

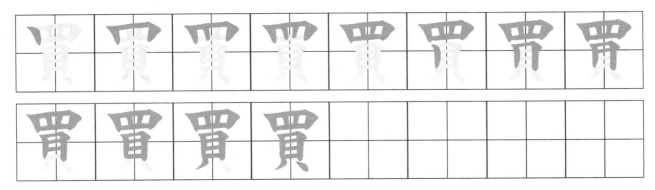

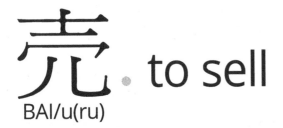 **to sell**

BAI/u(ru)

During Japan's period of high economic growth in the 1970s and 1980s, Japan was known to 売る *uru* (sell) good-quality, economical items all over the world. Today, 売 買 *baibai* (sales and purchases) have become more difficult, but doing *baibai* still stimulates the Japanese economy!

 Radical: 士   Number of strokes: seven

BUTSU, MOTSU/mono

(tangible) things

物 もの *mono* (thing) is used to designate many things, especially tangible ones, without having to name them. For example, 食べ物 た もの *tabemono* is "food" (literally things to eat) and 飲み物 の もの *nomimono* is "drinks" (literally things to drink). Japanese women still wear 着物 きもの *kimono* (literally things to wear, clothes), which are traditional Japanese clothes, for special occasions.

Radical: 牛   Number of strokes: eight

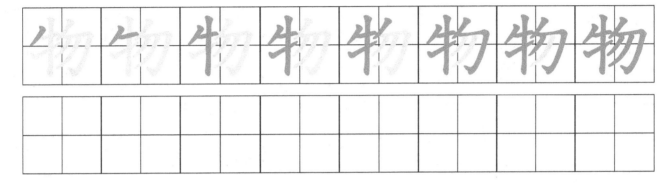

SHUTSU, SUI/ de(ru), da(su)

to depart, exit

This kanji is like two mountains (山) stacked up, but as shown below, the middle vertical line runs from the top to the bottom as one line. You will see this kanji in train stations, parking garages, and at building exits. Look for the sign 出口 でぐち *deguchi* (exit). It also indicates departure when combined with the kanji *hatsu*: 出発 しゅっぱつ *shuppatsu*. You will see this sign in any airport in Japan.

Radical: 山   Number of strokes: five

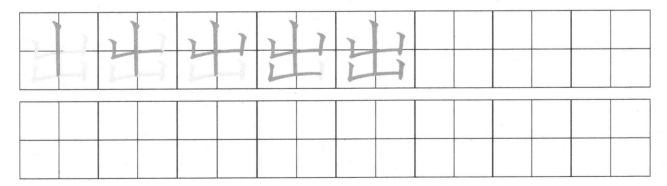

to enter

NYŪ/hai(ru)

This kanji is very simple to write, having only two strokes. It came from the shape of a con-ical hat. 入る *hairu* はい means "to enter," usually through an 入口 *iriguchi* いりぐち (entrance), while 入れる *ireru* い means to "put something into something." Don't confuse this with 人 (person, people), as these two kanji look alike! When you write 入, you start from the shorter left line.

 Radical: 入 Number of strokes: two

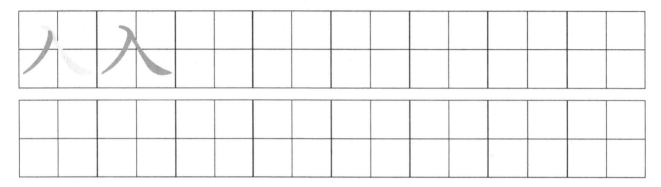

book, origin, root

HON/moto

Have you mastered the kanji for "tree"? Yes? Then all you have to do is add a small line that will serve as the root of the tree. As shown earlier, if you add the kanji for "sun," you will get 日本 *nihon*, にほん the "origin of the sun" (that is, the rising sun, which refers to Japan). Another meaning is "book." Books provide us with the basis of knowledge. When this kanji is com-bined with the kanji for "shop," we get 本店 *hon'ten* (main store). ほんてん

 Radical: 木 Number of strokes: five

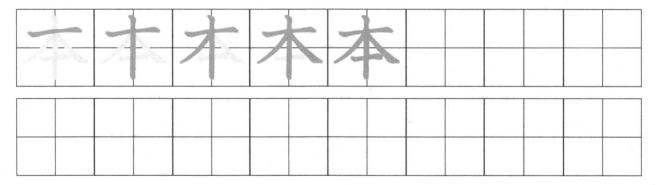

KOKU/kuni

country

国 *kuni* was once used to designate a province, and we can see traces of its historical meaning in the name of an island called 四国 *Shikoku* (four provinces). When you are out of the country, you are in a 外国 *gaikoku* (foreign county). In 1937, Yasunari Kawabata published his famous novel, 雪国 *Yukiguni* (*Snow Country*).

 Radical: 口 　　　　　　　　　　　Number of strokes: eight

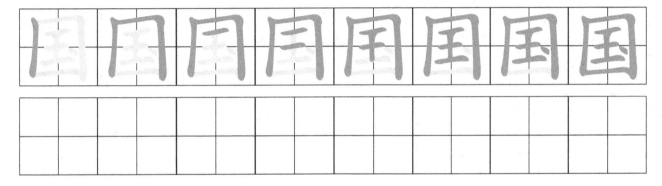

TEN/mise

store, shop

We have already seen this kanji combined with the kanji for "book," as 本店 *hon'ten* (main store). The common word for "bookstore" is 書店 *shoten*. If you want to dine out for a special occasion, you can find a good お店 *omise* (a general term for stores, shops, and restaurants) through a business directory!

 Radical: 广 　　　　　　　　　　　Number of strokes: eight

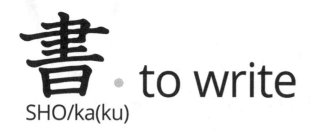 · to write

SHO/ka(ku)

Can you guess how to write this kanji? It may not be the easiest kanji to write, but if you follow the stroke order, you will think, "Oh, it's not so bad." 書く *kaku* is a basic verb meaning "to write." We also find this kanji quite naturally in the kanji for calligraphy, 書道 *shodō*, which means "the way of writing."

 Radical: 曰　　　　　　　　Number of strokes: ten

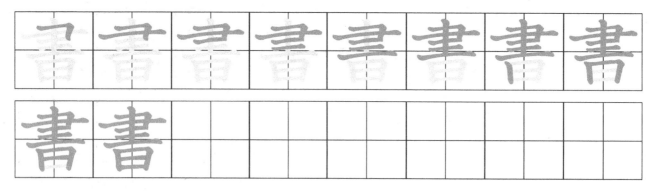

 · tea

CHA, SA

You should absolutely know this kanji! Japan is a country of *cha* (tea), which is generally referred to as お茶 *ocha*. People enjoy many kinds of tea in Japan, and you can get a wide variety of *ocha*, even from vending machines.

Tea is also an important part of 茶道 *sadō* or *chadō* (the way of tea), which is a tranquil process to calm your mind. If you have not done it, I hope you try it!

 Radical: 艹　　　　　　　　Number of strokes: nine

 time

JI/toki

 Radical: 日

Number of strokes: ten

This kanji can be divided into two parts. On the left you see the sun 日, and on the right you see the kanji for temple 寺. Notice that the sun 日 serves as the radical for this kanji and thus is smaller and skinnier than the regular kanji. When you are busy, you don't have 時間 *jikan* (time). You can add a number to 時 to indicate "o'clock." For example, do you work from 八時 *hachiji* (8:00) to 五時 *goji* (5:00)?

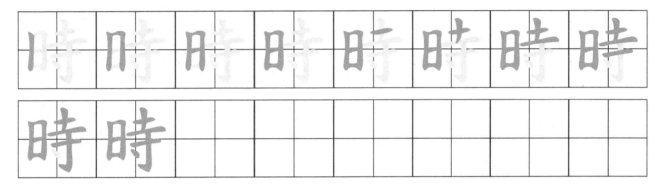

寺 temple

JI/tera

 Radical: 寸

Number of strokes: six

When you visit Japan, you may notice there are many 寺 *tera* (temples). When you go to Kyoto, you may be amazed by the stunning beauty of the different temples: 清水寺 *Kyomizu-dera*; 金閣寺 *Kinkaku-ji*, which showcases the Golden Pavilion; and 銀閣寺 *Ginkaku-ji*, where you can take a pleasant stroll in the peaceful garden.

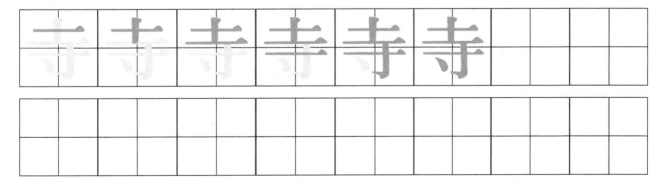

紙
SHI/kami

paper

The radical of this kanji is on the left and means "thread." The Japanese traditional

paper art, origami, contains this kanji; it's written as 折り紙 おがみ *origami*, which literally means "folding paper." If you add the kanji for "hand" to this kanji, the word

becomes 手紙 てがみ *tegami* (letter). Although social media are convenient, it is considered

more cultured and elegant to write a letter, which is 手紙を書く てがみ か *tegami (w)o kaku* in Japanese.

Radical: 糸

Number of strokes: ten

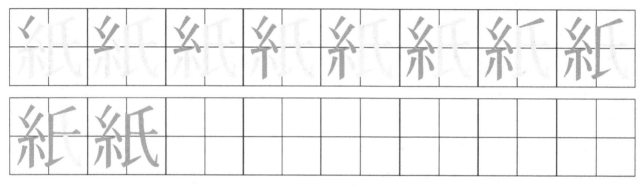

to live, birth

生きる い *ikiru* means "to live." It can also be read *umu* 生む う (to give birth) or *umareru*

生まれる う (to be born). Preceded by the kanji for "person," the meaning becomes life

in general — that is, 人生 じんせい *jinsei*.

生
SHŌ, SEI/i(kiru),
u(mareru), u(mu)

Radical: 生

Number of strokes: five

年 . year

NEN/toshi

Unlike in English, a year is preceded by numbers in Japanese. So, instead of saying "the year 2019," we would write 2019 年 (ねん) *nisen jūkyūnen.* So, for example, June 28, 2019, would be 2019年6月28日. When you arrive in Japan, you have to fill out a customs form in which you are asked to provide 生 年 月 日 (せいねんがっぴ) *seinen.gappi* (birth, year, month, day) — that is, your date of birth.

Radical: 干

Number of strokes: six

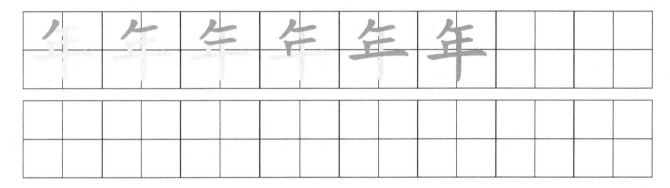

名 . name

MEI, MYŌ/
na

Combining *na* with the kanji meaning "before" or "front" (前 (まえ) *mae*), you can construct the word for "name": 名前 (なまえ) *namae.* 大 名 (だいみょう) *daimyō* (literally big name) was a rank reserved for Japanese feudal lords. During a trip to Japan, you may notice that many gift shops carry local products from their region, and refer to these products as 名物 *meibutsu* (famous things).

Radical: 口

Number of strokes: six

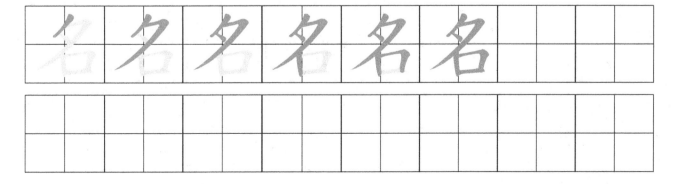

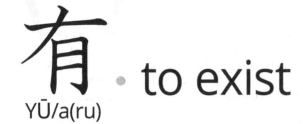 · to exist

YŪ/a(ru)

Pronounced 有る *aru*, this kanji means "to have" or "there is."

This verb is specifically used for inanimate objects, as in 木が有る *ki ga aru* (there are trees). For an animate (living) being, we use the verb *iru*, which has the same meaning in English; for example, 犬 がいる *Inu ga iru* (There is a dog). Combining *aru* with the previous kanji, 名 (name), you can make the word for "famous," 有名 *yūmei*.

 Radical: 月

Number of strokes: six

 · light

KŌ/hikari, hika(ru)

We need 光 *hikari* (light) physically and metaphorically. One of the high-speed trains, or *shinkansen*, was given this luminous name. Many plants use 日光 *nikkō* (sunlight) to grow.

光 Radical: 儿

Number of strokes: six

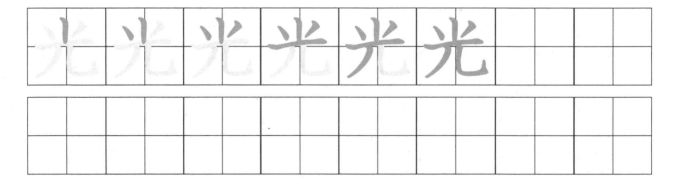

road, way, path

DŌ/michi

This kanji occupies a central place in the collective imagination of the people of Northeast Asia. It is the Chinese dao, the way, the path that must be followed to attain wisdom. As a result, this kanji is associated with many sports or artistic practices such as 書道 shodō (calligraphy), 茶道 sadō (the way of tea), けん道 kendō (the way of the sword), ぶし道 bushidō (the way of the samurai), and so on. 道 michi is a general term for "road," and 道にまよう michi ni mayou means losing your way, or "getting lost" in colloquial English.

Radical: 辶   Number of strokes: twelve

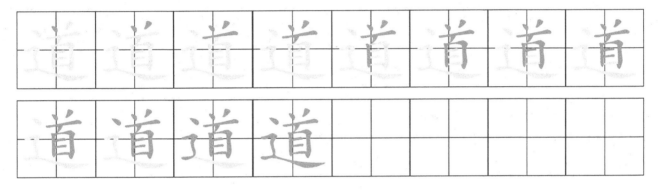

sky, emptiness

KŪ/kara, sora

空 sora (the sky) brings us whimsical charms: blue sky, dark cloudy sky, sky with fluffy clouds, and other variations. 青空 aozora (a blue sky) may make you feel happy, but 雨空 amazora (a rainy sky) looks gloomy. Japanese people admire the beauty of Mt. Fuji, Fujisan, with its snowy summit under the blue sky. If being contemplative or romantic is not your cup of tea, you might like something more active, like 空手 karate (literally empty hand)!

Radical: 穴   Number of strokes: eight

港 ● port

KŌ/minato

The modern port of Yokohama is called *Minato Mirai*, which means the port of the future. It's next to a very pretty harbor, where a big fireworks event is organized every summer. If you're not afraid of crowds, it's worth seeing! Combining this kanji with the kanji for "sky," you get くうこう

空 港 *kukō* (literally sky port), in other words, "airport." When you get なりたこくさいくうこう

to Japan, you might arrive at 成田国際空港 *Narita Kokusai Kūkō* (Narita International Airport).

 Radical: 氵   Number of strokes: twelve

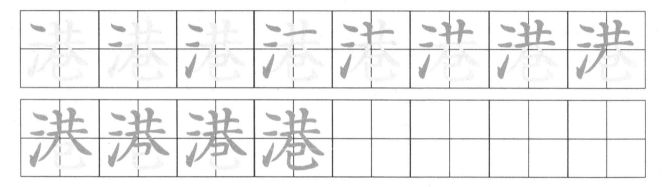

神 ● god, gods

SHIN, JIN/
kami

You may know that Japanese people tend to be polytheistic. しんとう

theistic. According to 神 道 *Shinto* (Shintoism), 神 *kami* (gods) are present everywhere: in trees, rivers, mountains, rocks, and so on. When students want to pass entrance examinations, they may pray to the かみ

神 さま *kamisama* (gods).

 Radical: 礻   Number of strokes: nine

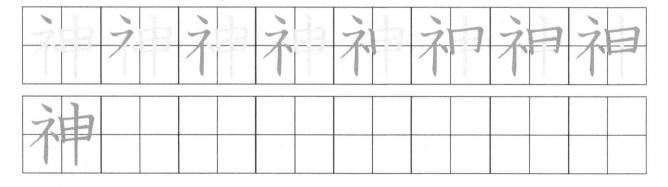

company, shrine

SHA, JA/
yashiro

Are you planning to work for a Japanese 会 社 *kaisha* (company)? In that case, you will have かいしゃ

to learn about 日 本 社 会 *nihon.shakai* (Japanese society). When you look for tranquility in にほんしゃかい

big cities, you will find it in a 神 社 *jinja* (shrine). These are typically quiet and surrounded じんじゃ

by nature, even if they're in the middle of a metropolitan area.

Radical: ネ

Number of strokes: seven

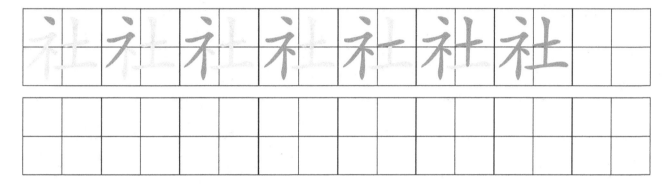

craftsmanship, skill

KŌ, KU/
takumi

This kanji looks very simple, having only three lines. If you are studying engineering, that's 工学

kōgaku. If something is made artificially, it's 人 工 的 *jinkōteki* (artificial). From this kanji, you じんこうてき

can also form the word 工 人 *kōjin* (craftsman, artisan). Some Japanese artisans have the title こうじん

of Living National Treasure that celebrates their skills and accomplishments.

Radical: 工

Number of strokes: three

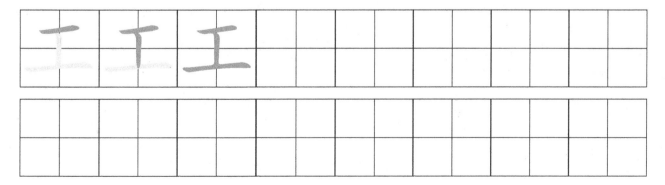

to study, to learn

<ruby>学<rt>まな</rt></ruby>

Learning never ends in one's life. The word 学ぶ *manabu* is the general term for "to learn." When you look at this kanji, can you see the kanji for "child" under the top part? It looks like a child under a roof. This kanji is found in compounds that suggest learning, such as <ruby>大 学<rt>だいがく</rt></ruby> *daigaku* (university, college) and <ruby>学 生<rt>がくせい</rt></ruby> *gakusei* (student).

GAKU/mana(bu)

Radical: 子

Number of strokes: eight

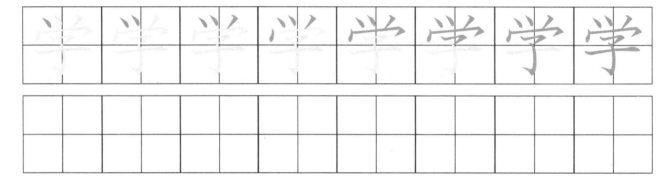

letter, character

字

Like *gaku*, this character also contains the kanji for "child," which is 子. You will see this kanji in the compound for *kanji* <ruby>漢 字<rt>かんじ</rt></ruby>, which means "characters of Han."

JI/aza

Radical: 子

Number of strokes: six

KAI, E

drawing, painting

In this kanji, we find the radical for "thread" on the left side. If you're interested in Japanese prints, you've probably heard of the woodblock prints, called うきよ絵 *ukiyoe* (images of the floating world), by Hokusai or Hiroshige.

Radical: 糸   Number of strokes: twelve

BYŌ/ega(ku),

ka(ku)

to draw

This kanji can be pronounced *ega-ku* or *ka-ku* (to draw). Redundantly, we also say 絵を描く *e (w)o kaku* (draw a drawing).

Radical: 扌   Number of strokes: eleven

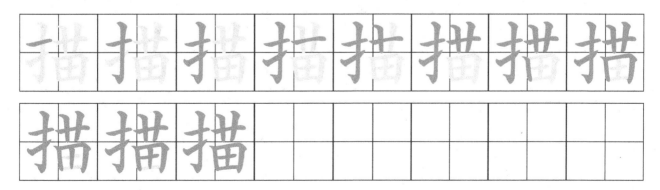

to live, inhabit

JŪ/su(mu)

A Japanese person may ask you, "お住まいはどちらですか" *osumai wa dochira desu ka?* (Where do you live?). To respond, you would use the verb 住む *sumu* (live) in your answer. When you purchase a cell phone, you will be asked to write your 住所 *jūsho* (address) in the agreement form.

Radical: 亻   Number of strokes: seven

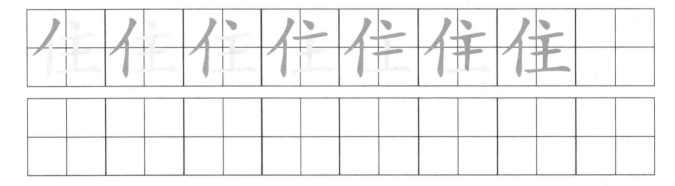

place, location

SHO/tokoro

The word 所 *tokoro* is a general word that refers to a place (or places). 場所 *basho* is also used to refer to a place or location. Taking a closer look at this kanji, you can see it is composed of two parts; the radical on the left means "door."

Radical: 戸   Number of radicals: eight

order, a number

Have you heard the word *ichiban*? It means "number one" or "best," and is an adverb used to express a superlative, just as you would use –est in English. *Ban* is used to rank something by adding a number to it. For example, 一番 *ichiban* is first, 二番 *niban* second, 三番 *san'ban* third, and so on.

 Radical: 田   Number of strokes: twelve

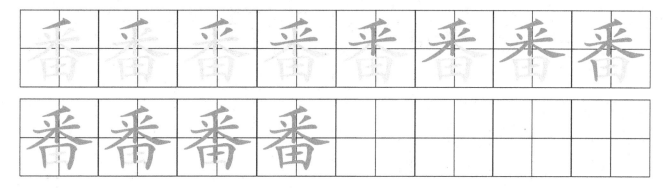

white

Does this kanji remind you of another kanji? You may remember that it looks like the sun 日 you saw earlier. The only difference is in the little nail-like line on its top. When you create this kanji, you start by drawing the small line at the top. 白い *shiroi* means "white." This kanji also suggests clean and clear. For example, 白紙 *hakushi* means "white paper," but it also indicates a clean slate, as in 白紙にもどす *hakushi ni modosu* (to start anew).

 radical: 白   number of strokes: five

 **black**

KOKU/kuro

Can you visualize an octopus dancing under the sea in this kanji? 黒 い *kuroi* is an adjective that describes something black or dark. 黒 い 髪 *kuroi kami* means black hair or dark hair. 黒 板 *kokuban*, literally "black board," refers (unsurprisingly) to a "blackboard."

 Radical: 黒   Number of strokes: eleven

 **red**

SEKI/aka

赤 *aka* (red) is a color traditionally appreciated by the Japanese, and is considered celebratory and energetic. It is found in the shrines and on the national flag, with the sun being red in the Japanese imagination. 赤 い *akai* is a general term (adjective) to describe something as being red. 赤 道 *sekidō* (literally red road) refers to the equator.

 Radical: 赤   Number of strokes: seven

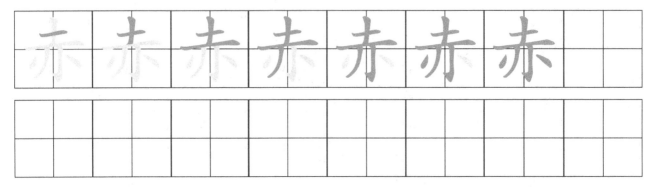

青 · blue

SEI/ao

Radical: 青

Number of strokes: eight

In Japan, this kanji has long meant both green and blue. For example,
even today, "lawn" is described with 青 い *aoi* (あお), instead of using the
word *midori* (green). But *aoi* is a general term for blue. For example,
青 い 海 *aoi umi* (あお うみ) is "blue ocean" and 青 い 花 *aoi hana* (あお はな) is "blue flower."
The color blue also suggests something that is not quite mature. For
example, 青 年 *seinen* (せいねん) means "young people."

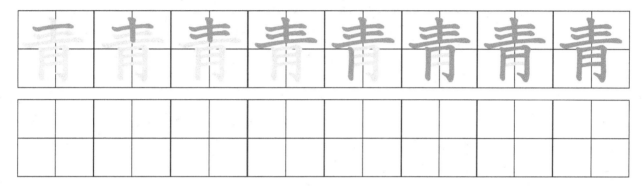

Appendix

Blank Grids for Extra Practice

Japanese Character Writing For Dummies

About the Author

Hiroko Chiba is a professor of Asian Studies (Japanese Studies) at DePauw University in Greencastle, Indiana. She teaches all levels of Japanese language and Japanese culture and directs the Japanese language program there. Her professional life revolves around various interests related to language teaching and learning. Her research interests include language acquisition, cross-cultural studies of aesthetic perceptions, and Japanese science fiction anime. She has authored and co-authored a wide variety of research studies domestically and internationally. She has also served as the president for the Association of Indiana Teachers of Japanese. Hiroko loves teaching and enjoys offering action-packed classes every day. When she has free time, she is a devoted student of yoga and an admirer of **kawaii** (*cute*) products such as Hello Kitty and companion robots like Aibo. Hiroko received a PhD in Educational Psychology from the University of Illinois at Urbana-Champaign.

Dedication

To my former, present, and future students.

Author's Acknowledgments

Many thanks to the editors — Lindsay Lefevere, Chrissy Guthrie, and Marylouise Wiack — for patiently having worked with me. I'm much obliged to them. A big thank you to Dr. Charles Andrews who served as a technical reviewer. His comments were helpful and thoughtful. And last, but not least, I would like to thank my family members in Japan who helped me pursue this project in many important ways.

Publisher's Acknowledgments

Executive Editor: Lindsay Sandman Lefevere

Editorial Project Manager and Development Editor: Christina N. Guthrie

Copy Editor: Marylouise Wiack

Technical Editor: Dr. Charles Andrews

Production Editor: Mohammed Zafar Ali

Cover Photos: © anants/iStockphoto